The Science of Self Realisation Guide Book Printed in England 2017

·Contents·

·The Peace Invocation·

Om.
All those that are invisible are filled by Brahman,
all those that are visible are also fully permeated by Brahman.
The whole universe has come out of the whole Brahman.
Brahman is still full, although the whole universe has come out of It.

0 Gods, with our ears may we hear what is auspicious.
With our eyes may we see what is auspicious, o ye worshipful ones.
May we enjoy the life allotted to us by the Gods,
offering them the activities of our strong limbs and body as a life-long praise.

May Brahman protect us both together.
May He nourish us both together.
May we work together with great energy.
May our study be vigorous and effective.
May we not hate each other.

Om Peace! Peace! Peace!

·Svetasvatara Upanishad·

A Note from Satguru Sri Ramana Devi

It is my honour to introduce you to Svetasvatara Upanishad. I have compiled all 113 verses along with: direction on the verse meaning, a commentary from the heart, direction on the verse's main point, a set of questions to stimulate study, discussion and awareness of the teachings, to develop your inner knowledge so you may put the teachings into practice in your daily life; and finally, a thought for the day to reflect on for each verse.

The direction written for each verse is a conscious directive from my higher mind to yours, to enable you to cognitively experience the Upanishadic verse simply and without confusion. It is a clear and concise guidance towards your enlightenment and the steps needed to be taken methodically and scientifically to reach home with our Supreme Consciousness. On writing the heart translation it was my intention to generate an atmosphere of love and devotion in your heart, mind and body. I wished to invoke an awareness in you of your own Divinity, and therefore support you in the experience of God wherever you are, and whenever you read the translation. The main point of the verse such as humility, compassion etc, will aid you in deepening your knowledge of these Divine attributes.

The questions attached to each verse are designed to wake up aspects of yourself to the specific teachings from Svetasvatara. It is the intention of the Svetasvatara to remind you of your need to cultivate your individual Self and a relationship with God, and to practice yoga.

You are also reminded of your absolute need for a Guru - a knower of Brahman - to guide you towards the light and away from the darkness. Without a Guru, an individual can become lost and therefore never reach home in his/her present incarnation.

This Guidebook has been designed to lead you from darkness to light. It is the intention set at the beginning of this study to guide you effortlessly and comprehensively, and if done thoroughly, this Guidebook is guaranteed to take you home to Self Realisation. The Svetasvatara Upanishad verses are all you will ever need to awaken you to the inner process of Self Realisation.

With love
Ramana

· An Introduction to Svetasvatara Upanishad ·

The Svetasvatara Upanishad is a short Upanishad consisting of only 113 mantras (sacred verses) divided into six chapters. It belongs to the Krsnayajurveda. It gets its name from the sage Svetasvatara who is said to have taught it to his disciples. According to Sankarananda the word means one who has controlled his senses. (Sveta = pure and Asva = Indiyas or senses). The word signifies the greatness of the teacher.

Many of the mantras within Svetasvatara Upanishad are quoted by commentators in support of their doctrines. This shows what an important position of authority it held in the eyes of the great commentators. It does not advocate any particular system of orthodox philosophy, as elaborated in the Darsanas (systems of philosophy) or in their expositions. There are passages in this Upanishad which are allied in thought to Dvaita (dualism), Visistadvaita (non-dualism), Advaita (qualified non-dualism) and other branches of Vedanta. Sankhya and Yoga ideas find a prominent place in certain verses. It lays equal emphasis on Jnana, Bhakti and other paths of spiritual life. The various aspects of Godhead find their natural place in it and adjust themselves to each other without any conflict. If in certain passages it is Vedic in language and conception, in others it is also Puranic in expression and presentation. In fact , it would seem to be an attempt of a great synthetic mind to reconcile the various conflicting views, philosophical and religious, which were current at the time of its compostion. It reminds us of a similar, but a more popular attempt in this direction, made by Bhagavan Sri Krishna in the Gita. The modern student will therefore do well to approach the study of this work in the same broad and reverent spirit in which he approaches the study of Gita, unfettered by conventions and predjudices.

· An Introduction to Satguru Sri Ramana Devi ·

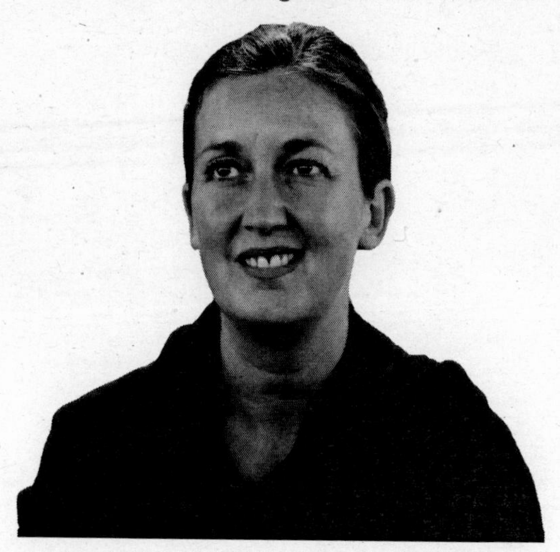

The Upanishads, ancient Hindu scriptures, stress the importance of having a Guru on any spiritual path. The Chandogya Upanishad illustrates the necessity of the Guru by asking us to imagine that we are blindfolded and taken to some remote place, completely lost with no idea where we are, struggling to find our way home. Without help, we will not be able to find our way- the path is too long, too difficult, too complex. Suddenly though, someone appears who knows the way, who can tell us, 'Your home is this way.' Filled with newfound courage and excitement, we can start to begin our journey home, safe in the knowledge that we are on the right path and we will reach our destination. That person who appears to us when we are lost in darkness and guides us home is the Guru.

Satguru Sri Ramana Devi is one such Guru. Sri Ramana Devi guides souls from the darkness into the light with her abundance of divine, unconditional love. Sri Ramana Devi loves every being that exists and helps all to be more aware of their True Divine Nature - that we are all an aspect of God.

Sri Ramana Devi is passionate about making God normal and accessible for people from all walks of life. She believes passionately that you do not have to renounce the world and meditate in a remote cave to have an experience of God and has made it her mission to make Self Realization normal in Western society.

In Sri Ramana Devi's presence one automatically feels a greater awareness of one's own True Nature - thoughts and feelings that normally plague us diminish and you are left with the most incredible experience of peace, bliss and comfort.

In Hinduism this experience is called 'darshan' (meaning to see or be seen by a holy person or deity) and it is highly treasured. Sri Ramana Devi's love is so powerful that even a few moments in her presence is enough to transform an individual.

The Upanishads state that the five signs of being in the presence of Satguru (Satguru means a true teacher) are: knowledge flourishes, sorrow diminishes; joy wells up without any reason, abundance dawns, all talents manifest. These are constant experiences of those who meet Sri Ramana Devi. Whenever you are in the presence of Sri Ramana Devi she is guiding you back home. Discussions with Sri Ramana Devi are never one dimensional - even if you are discussing something as simple as washing the dishes or planting a vegetable, Sri Ramana Devi is helping you to be more aware of your Self.

History of Satguru Sri Ramana Devi

When she was still a five year old schoolgirl, Sri Ramana Devi realised that she was not separate from God, and that everyone and everything was an aspect of God. Since that young age, Sri Ramana Devi has been helping people in any way possible to realise the Self. As a child, Sri Ramana Devi was known for being unusually kind and loving. Sri Ramana Devi is very down to earth and knew that in order to fully help people she needed to be able to empathise with what they were experiencing in life, and that this would help people to be able to build a connection with her. So, Sri Ramana Devi decided to have as many 'normal' human experiences as possible, so that she could fully relate to people and what they were going through. This included, in later life, getting married and having a family. So, whatever experiences you have had in your life, it is likely that Sri Ramana Devi has experienced them too.

When she was 18, Sri Ramana Devi decided to dedicate her life to helping others to be more aware of their True Nature. After searching for many years for a philosophy that matched her own innate knowledge, Sri Ramana Devi found that all the wisdom and knowledge that she felt, was mirrored in the ancient Hindu scriptures - particularly the Upanishads. Sri Ramana Devi began to promote Hindu philosophy as a path to realising the Self and stressed the importance of the ancient scriptures, in particular 'shruti' texts which are said to have been 'heard' by the sages in deep meditation rather than written.

Current Activities

Sri Ramana Devi moved to her current Ashram in Rossendale, Lancashire in 2009. During these years she trained a small group of devotees to be able to carry her message into the world and share with people the transformational power of divine love, so freely available from Sri Ramana Devi.

Sri Ramana Devi's Ashram is a vegan farm with over forty animals whom Sri Ramana Devi considers to be her best friends. Sri Ramana Devi is passionate about animal compassion and has set up projects to promote animal kindness and veganism/vegetarianism in society. Sri Ramana Devi knows that we are not our forms; we are all souls and equals and should treat each other with love, kindness and compassion. In Sri Ramana Devi's presence the animals at the farm experience transformations that are evident to all who meet them. Their love and gratitude to Sri Ramana Devi is obvious for all to see.

Sri Ramana Devi makes herself available to all who wish to come and experience the Self, and visit her at the Ashram. Sri Ramana Devi also travels both nationally and internationally, and is open to all.
For more opportunities as to how you can meet Sri Ramana Devi, please visit her **website: www.sriramanadevi.org**

·Studying The Science of Self Realisation Guidebook·

Sri Ramana Devi promotes the Upanishads, and in particular the Svetasvatara Upanishad, as total reflections of everything that she holds dear and knows to be true. Sri Ramana Devi shares of the beauty of the Svetasvatara Upanishad, and the incredible way in which it is able to transform the reader and enable them to experience their heart.

Sri Ramana Devi has translated this most beautiful of the Upanishads to make it more accessible for a modern audience. Sri Ramana Devi's translations of the ancient verses instantly connect the reader with their Divine Nature. Sri Ramana Devi wrote the verses previously from a solely Bhakti (the path of the heart and of devotion) perspective and they explored the individual soul's longing and yearning for oneness with God.

This Guidebook explores the verses further and includes a Jnani perspective. Jnani yoga is the path of knowledge and of the mind. Sri Ramana Devi teaches that for realization to occur one must utilize the heart, mind and body together to explore the nature of the Self. The Guidebook enables you to go deeper into the verses and gives you an awareness of your own Self and your relationship with God.

There are many ways in which you can study the verses. You can study the verses individually at home. You could incorporate studying the Upanishad into your daily spiritual practice, if you have one, or just set time aside to sit and study. You could focus on one verse per day, or perhaps you might like to focus on one verse for a week or more, perhaps one day you might like to study ten verses! The choice is yours and it is an individual decision as to what feels right for you.

You could set up a study group with friends and family. A group setting can bring you new awarenesses as you can often see your Self reflected back to you in the insights of others. Focused groups can build a high energy together, one of excitement, exploration and passion to uncover the truth of their Divine Nature!

You could go one step further and start a formal group. This is a great opportunity to spend time with like minded people - it is important in the world to have support on your spiritual path. It can feel very lonely at times and though this loneliness is ultimately a heartfelt desire to merge with God, the friendship and camaraderie of other spiritual seekers can help you to feel less alone. You may also find it easier to share yourself more openly with people that you do not know so well. Holding such a group is a wonderful opportunity to share your Self with others, and the boons that you receive from God when you share what you have received are bountiful.

If you are very passionate about the powerful impact of these verses and their translation then you could choose to help Sri Ramana Devi in her mission and share these Upanishads on a wider scale. Perhaps there is a group in society that you feel would really benefit from studying these verses and having an experience of their Self? You could start up a study group in a prison, a mental health facility, a university, a hospice/hospital, a women's centre - the list is endless. Such a group would give you a wonderful opportunity for Self awareness and Self knowledge. It is said that it is in the sharing that you are able to fully assimilate what you yourself have received; Sri Ramana Devi's devotees are testament to this truth!

If you would like any help and support in sharing Sri Ramana Devi's Upanishads with others please contact: **info@sriramanadevi.org**

The Guidebook

Chapters I - VI

·Chapter I·

Verse 1

Verse
'Hari om! The enquirers of Brahman converse (among each other). What is the cause? Is it Brahman? Whence are we born? By whom do we live? Where do we ultimately abide? By whom governed, in pains and pleasures, do we live our various conditions, 0 ye knowers of Brahman?'

JnaniYoga
It is imperative that we start our enquiry into our True Selves by asking the most fundamental questions. We must ask these questions first to ourselves, then to our Guru and ultimately to Brahman (God) himself. We must be willing to relinquish all control and perform the ultimate act of humility by honestly speaking the truth of our moment, right now, that we of ourselves have no idea who we are, why we exist and what our purpose is. This humility is the foundation on which our path of Self enquiry must rest upon, so that what follows must reach an open mind, prepared willingly by us for God. And, that it is through the Guru (knower of Brahman) and God that our answers will come. That we of ourselves are lost, and cannot find our way without the Guru's wisdom and light.

Bhakti Yoga
What is the reason for our very existence here in this world Brahman? Who are we to be here in this Maya, this illusory existence full of toils and troubles? Why

·Chapter I·

do we have to be here at all, to suffer pain gladly, but why, oh why, do we?

Are we to believe that there is something else? Another reason for our existence other than the pain and pleasure our five senses toil over day by day? Do we not need you more and more each day to serve you gladly to our heart's content? Do we not need you day by day to desire you, and only you? If not, why not, oh Brahman? What is the reason for being attached to this worldly body if not to be in service to you always? If not to lie beside you always filled with your warm embrace. Please serve our souls, please remember us, please never forget us, oh Brahman.

We need you to remind us. Our saving grace is for you to plant the seed of remembrance always in our hearts, always in our minds. Do we not reside here on this plane of existence only to serve, to serve a greater power than ourselves? Maybe we will never know. Remind us. Remember us. Remind us.

Karma Yoga HUMILITY
Humility is a creation from God to know who you are in every moment. It is the ability to find a light, playful, simple, childlike quality within. A quality that can see the humour in all things, and even see the unrealness of all manifestation. It is the capacity to look beyond the mask of the illusory world, to remove the veil of ignorance from our eyes and behold the Lord in all we see. We can see God in everything, but our serious nature withholds so much truth from us, as we hold onto control and painfully seek to keep attached to our fai:;:ade. We must remove this ignorance by seeing everything as God intended, as part of his Divine play. We are not here to suffer, we are here to journey on with faith and devotion until we reach a level place that we can call home.

Open your eyes, see the world like a child - with innocence, respect for the creator and reverence for his direction. This is a perfect world, we are playing a perfect role, designed by us and God together for our own good and the good of all.

Questions
1.Who is Brahman?
2.What is maya (illusory existence)?
3.What does it mean to suffer pain gladly?
4.What is the reason we exist?
5.What do our five senses toil over each day?
6.How can we serve Brahman?

·Chapter I·

7.Why do we need to desire Brahman?
8.Why are we attached to our worldly body?
9.How does Brahman remind us of who we are?
10.How can we cultivate humility?

Today: Carry the Upanishad verse in your pocket. Throughout the day read the verse to remind you that you only exist in every moment for God - your duty in this existence is to be of service.

Verse 2

Verse
'Time, inherent nature, law or necessity or chance or the elements or matter or a womb or a male, are to be considered as the cause. It is not a combination of these because of the existence of the Soul (Atman). The Soul (the Individual Soul) also is not free as he is under the sway of pleasure and pain.'

JnaniYoga
Once humility is cultivated within the soul, the soul must realise itself to be separate from all others, even from its previous births. It must realise its individuality to be able to identify its own personal karma - the unique culmination of actions that it must be freed from, the pleasures and pains it individually toils over repeatedly day after day. This must come next, so that the Guru can give instruction on how best this sadhaka can renounce the reality that has become so imbedded in its psyche.

Bhakti Yoga
The soul brings a variety of vasanas into this birth - no soul enters a body free from the toils of previous births. Why, oh why, oh Brahman, do we free ourselves from the bondage of you, such bondage is all a soul desires, to be tied to you for eternity. What a birth that would be! Can we ever be free, can we ever be free to know that our oneness is with you and nothing else? To be attached to such maya, such transitory experiences of male, of female, of womb, of form. I am indebted to your wisdom, your silent voice in the womb of my soul to give birth to such beauty, to such freedom as to know thy Self separate from the shackles of separative existence. Separate from the identification of the formed self to merge entirely into the body of the formless Self - to feel the realness of the formless Self, so no other self can I identify myself to be. Free me from this transitory gaze, allow my gaze to ever be with thee. I am you, you are me, we are free.

·Chapter I·

Karma Yoga
INDIVIDUALITY
Our karma separates us from each other. It is gift from God to enable us to see who we really are. It is a Divine boon to be given even just one moment of an individual experience. We spend many lives merged together in one unconscious soup of egoistic consciousness. It is our job to identify with, and understand, who we are. We cannot do this with confusion, doubt, mistrust. We have to lay ourselves open to our creator to show us who we really are. This starts with humility and an openness to face our Truth. There will always be apprehension that we will not like what we find, but it is with faith and devotion that we find the inner strength to allow our self to be submerged in Truth. It is in this Truth that we can see our True Self, and start the process of renunciation. We must renounce all that we are that is not Divine, one defect, one failing at a time. We must push through all of our resistances which will show themselves to us along the way, and spend time practicing focusing on what we find in ourselves to be Divine. The Divinity we see will take us home, and lead us through the darkness of ignorance and arrogance to more and more Truth. Our individuality is all that we have. It is that sense of 'me' that arises from an awareness within, a drive to know the absolute truth. I am. I am. I am.

Questions
1.What are vasanas?
2.Why does a soul not enter a body without the toils of previous births?
3.Why do souls free themselves from their attachment to Brahman?
4.What does it mean to be tied to Brahman for eternity?
5.Can a soul ever be free?
6.Why does a soul become attached to roles etc?
7.What is separative existence?
8.What is the formed self?
9.How can one merge into the body of the formless self?
10.How can we gaze with Brahman only?

Today: Spend time identifying yourself as formless - imagine you are not your gender, your age, your beliefs, your ideas, your imaginings. You are beyond all matter, all form.

Verse 3

Verse
'They who practiced meditation realised or saw as the cause of creation, the power of God (Devatma-Sakti) hidden in his own qualities (gunas)

·Chapter I·

which alone rules over all these causes (enumerated in verse two), beginning with time and ending with the Individual Soul.'

JnaniYoga

The third step in realisation after humbly surrendering to Guru/God, and seeing your separativeness from all else, is to meditate on your True Nature to practice realising that within all is an Atman, created by God for God, that lives deep within your being, beyond your form and actions. It is the cause of all your pains and pleasures. It created itself to know itself as real. Within the very fabric of your very nature is God.

Bhakti Yoga

You are everywhere, oh Brahman, in everything at all times. How could man have lost sight of such power, such greatness? From time to the Individual Soul you reside within, quietly emitting such wisdom, such knowledge, such awareness. Such is the realisation of the Soul to waken up to the knowingness that it is you inside that they experience. When oneness is felt within time, oh my heart yearns for more to know you, to experience you, to have you be with me in time, in nature, in man, in woman. Be with me always. May I always know that it is you, always, always you.

Karma Yoga
ATMAN

I am that. That is me. There is no other existence, but myself. This is the realisation of the Atman. The Atman is an essence of Brahman, the Supreme Consciousness. It is the absolute experience of 'I'. Not the egoic 'I' that feels inadequate and therefore small. But the big 'I', that recognises its need for Brahman, and honours the principle that only in experiencing itself can it ever know where it came from, and where it is going to. The Atman is humble and separate from all egoism and its activity. It is peaceful, real, truthful, calm, loving, open and compassionate. It is the Truthful part of all human nature. The consciousness of the mind, the heart of the soul. It cannot be destroyed or created. It is a presence within, that once realised can take you on a journey of absolute discovery. The Atman fuels itself daily on the love of God. It merges constantly throughout the day, in every moment, with the Divine. Love pushes it on to find its way home. It is a relentless organism within everyone that feels whole, alive and free. Once experienced it can never be forgotten.

Questions

1.What does it mean that Brahman is everywhere and in everything?
2.How did man lose sight of the power and greatness of Brahman?

·Chapter I·

3.How does Brahman reside within, emitting wisdom and knowledge?
4.How can a soul realise Brahman is what they are experiencing?
5.Describe the experience of Brahman in time.
6.What does it feel like to have a heart that yearns?
7.How can you help yourself to always know that it is Brahman in everything that you experience?
8.Do you have experiences of your Atman?
9.Can you see the difference between the 'I's mentioned?
10.Describe the experiences of your Átman.

Today: Look at a watch or a clock and be aware of time. In your awareness of time feel the power of Brahman reminding you that you are never alone.

Verse 4

Verse
'We understand him as a wheel which has one telly with a triple tyre with sixteen end parts, fifty spokes, twenty counter spokes, with six sets of eights, which has one rope of various forms, which has three different roads or paths and which has one revolution for two traces.'

JnaniYoga
Then you must lay yourself wide open to have all your preconceived ideas, beliefs and thoughts challenged, broken down , dismantled, so that you can practice renunciation. Renunciation is an inner path, one where everything believed to be real about you, God, the universe can be rebuilt from your True Self. All concepts, philosophies and everything of the mind must be challenged.

Bhakti Yoga
I am not as I appear to be today, I am not as I appear to be any day. I am not as I appear. Appearance is deceptive. Don't look for me in what you see, you will not find me there. Don't look for me in what you feel, you will not find me there.
Don't look for me in what you do, you will not find me there. You say, 'If not in what you see, what you feel, or what you do, pray where are you?' I say, 'Look for me inside yourself, you will always find me there.' I sat awhile and waited there, I waited there awhile. And now I know in all I sat, I sat awhile with you.

Karma Yoga
RENUNCIATION
Renunciation is an open acknowledgement that you are a vessel for God. Your purpose is to serve only God. It is your Divine goal to realise all that you are; that

·Chapter I·

is good, kind, compassionate, loving. All the qualities and attributes inside your being that are an aspect of God are to be realised. For this to happen you must also realise that there are aspects of yourself that have forgotten your True Nature, and can manifest in many fearful ways, such as lust, greed, anger, desire, fear etc. These manifestations of godlessness are to be faced and ultimately conquered. You must realise that these are not true representations of who you really are. This process of letting go and surrendering your defects of character to the God of your choosing is called renunciation. There are two ways to practice renunciation. One is to completely renounce the world and live in an ashram. For this to be effective you have to have no debts and no relationships with family members, and then you can completely focus on your Self and let go of all your desires and attachments. This is the hardest route, but also the fastest. The second option is to renounce whilst still actively seeking worldly attachments. This choice is easier, but can only work when devotion to God (Bhakti) is cultivated above all else. You would have to place God first in your life, and then all other relationships would be secondary. Once renunciation begins you will start to experience yourself as an open vessel for God's love to pour in. Enlightenment will occur gradually and effortlessly. This is the way of Self Realisation on a conscious level.

Questions
1.What does it mean to appear to be something or someone?
2.Why is appearance deceptive?
3.Why are you not to be found in your feelings, actions and how you see things?
4.What is prayer?
5.Where are you inside yourself?
6.What does it mean to sit awhile with God?
7.What are preconceived ideas, beliefs and thoughts?
8.What does it mean to challenge, dismantle your preconceived beliefs and ideas?
9.What is renunciation?
10.How can you rebuild your beliefs, ideas and thoughts?

Today: Sit down as often as possible and stop looking, feeling and doing Onana, bhakti and karma) and be with me a while.

Verse 5

Verse
'We understand him as a river of five streams from five sources, impetuous and crooked, whose waves are the five pranas or vital breaths, whose original source is five-fold perception {the mind), which has five whirlpools,

·Chapter I·

which is impelled by the velocity of the fivefold misery or pain, which is divided by the five kinds of misery and which has five turnings or branches.'

JnaniYoga
It is now that we face our first and ultimate challenge. That it is in our sensory experiences that we will find Truth, God, Love. The answers that we seek are not separate from the pain that separates us from knowing the Truth. It is in the reality of misery and pain that the truth may unfold. So we close our eyes and therefore our mind fills with all of our sensory experiences and we sit, we be in the presence of all that has caused us pain and suffering. And within this pain the truth emerges like a light being turned on in a darkened room.

Bhakti Yoga
We understand him not, we understand nothing of what is real, nothing of what is imagined, we absorb so much and yet we absorb nothing at all. What do we intake into our being? What is the use of these sensory experiences? Of what use are we with them? Of what use are we without them? Do we have a use? What is the need that arises like a storm, erupting inside our being at any moment, exploding our senses until we can stand no more. Is this need met by desires, by nature, by anything real? Can we ever feel the need as it was designed to be? Are we destined to journey through miles and miles of trenches, trenches of lost needs, mistaken beliefs, of what we think we should receive?! Are we to live out our lives ignorant to the pleas of our soul? Our pleas of mercy, of forgiveness. Forgive us, oh Brahman the merciful, forgive us our sins. Forgive us our forever wanderings here and there. Forgive us for forgetting who we really are from this moment to the next blissful moment, in baited anticipation of your love, your warmth, your tenderness. Forgive us for forgetting you, for not knowing you, for finding you in places where you are not, and not finding you where you are. Here always in our hearts. Our hearts are one with you, oh Brahman, our hearts are one.

Karma Yoga
TRUTH
The Ultimate Truth is Divine, beautiful, mesmerising and takes your breath away. It awakens you to your heart, and the calling inside, beckoning you back home to your Supreme Creator. It is a quiet, simple knowingness that all that is and ever will be, is truly for good and for your own evolution . The process of realising your True Nature, and finding 'Truths' within that enable you to grow and evolve into a better, more advanced version of yourself. Truth is an advanced consciousness, it is more than the opposite of telling lies on a superficial level.

·Chapter I·

On a deeper, more meaningful level it is knowing who you are, why you are here and what you must do in any moment. It is possible to experience Truth without Full Realisation to have occurred and it is this that you are striving to experience more and more. More and more experiences of Truth keep you in the energy of enlightenment and provide you with the strength, courage and wisdom required to move forward along your path of Realisation.

Questions
1.What does it mean to understand something?
2.What does it mean to absorb so much and yet nothing is really absorbed?
3.What do we intake into our being?
4.What are sensory experiences?
5.Do we have a use?
6.What is need?
7.Do desires meet our needs?
8.How can we receive forgiveness for our sins?
9.Why do we forget God?
10.How can we feel our hearts at one with Brahman?

Today: Spend time breathing slowly, deeply into an awareness of your spiritual heart. Whilst your awareness rests within your heart, allow any sensory experiences to flow past your being with ease and recognise the contentment you feel as your awareness of your spiritual heart meets your every need.

Verse 6

Verse
'In this Infinite wheel of Brahman in which everything lives and rests, the pilgrim Soul or the reincarnating Self is whirled about when he thinks that he and the Supreme Ruler are different or separate. He attains immortality when he is blessed or favoured by him.'

JnaniYoga
After you have pushed past your desires and sensory experiences and connected with your True Nature, you will feel an absolute pain in your heart, like no other. An ache, a yearning, a sense of being pulled away from your ego towards something unknown, and yet familiar. It is this pain that will drive you further, closer to the Truth, to an ever greater awareness of God. You will not recognise this ache

·Chapter I·

at first, you may feel it is wrong or inappropriate, but, I assure you that this ache in your heart is normal and a constant reminder of where you are going, and how much you desperately want to reach this unknown place called home.

Bhakti Yoga
Around and around I look for you, I look for you in places of pleasure and places of pain. I look for you here and I look for you there! Why are you not there when I am looking? Where are you hiding? Why is it that I cannot find you? I am looking within you, in everything you see I am looking with you. I see everything you see, I am in everything you see. In all the moments you look I am there with you, holding you, guiding you gently towards the light of knowledge that I am always there with you. Even when I am not there, I am there. I cannot help but be there.

KarmaYoga
NEED
So many people seem to need people, places and things. Transitory experiences, far too many to separate them from each other. All are merging, enmeshed into an inner atmosphere of fullness and activity. The mind, the heart and the body become so full that you can no longer imagine your Atman calling you home, you can no longer feel the hungry ache for God in your heart. The need for God is real, necessary and absolutely vital for your path. It is compulsory that you are able to spend time in the day connecting with a deep yearning, a sadness, a lust for Divinity. Divinity is felt when you recognise the need, and allow God into your being. The heart feels alive, the mind feels quiet and the body feels still. All parts of your being are aligned and open to be a worthy vessel for God to reside within, and for you to carry out his Divine plan for you.

Questions
1.What does it mean to feel separate from God?
2.How can you attain immortality by being blessed or favoured by him?
3.How do you look for God?
4.How do you look for God in places of pleasure and pain?
5.Why can you not find God when you look for him?
6.How does God hide from you?
7.Describe how it feels to ache for God.
8.Explain your heart, and how it feels when you yearn.
9.How does God be in everything you are, see and do?
10.What does it mean that there is God and there is you?

Today: Practice knowing that wherever you are, I am there too.

·Chapter I·

Verse 7

Verse
'This is verily declared as the Supreme Brahman. In that is the triad. It is the firm support. It is the indestructible - by knowing what is therein, the knowers of Brahman become devoted to Brahman, merge themselves in it, and are liberated from birth.'

JnaniYoga
On realising the nature of the Divine is within you, you must explore the nature of the Divine. You must research, investigate what this nature is. What does it mean to be Divine? You must break it down, analyse and dissect all that you can find out about what it actually means to be Divine. How can you ever be something if you are not absolutely certain of what it is that you are actually trying to be? An enquiring mind must engage now in methodical observations of everything it believes, or knows, about Divinity.

Bhakti Yoga
I know the difference between the three worlds, I know there is a difference but, I wonder, where will I find you in them? Will I find you at all? I look around so much and wonder why I look around at all. I look inside, outside, over here, over there, I really am looking everywhere. But where to find you I don't know, I don't know. I'm in the you, I'm in the me, I'm in the there, I'm in the he, I'm in the we, I'm in the it, I'm in the where at all. I looked in there and I looked inside but still I couldn't see. I looked for you in all those things but still I could not see. I'm looking now, just like you said, in everything and more. I'm looking now, just now I think I'm looking and I can see. You're in the more, the place beyond far reaching from the shore. The shore of life is cold and bare, I could not see you there. But when I stretched my gaze a while past the shore, I experienced a vastness of abundant love and there I find you now. The ocean of your blissful Self is now and ever more imprinted on the heart of mine and will forever be. I know now that you were always there, inside my very Self, and all the while I looked around I could not see you there. I cried and I cried an enormous tear to know you more and more. And when that tear departed mine, it fell upon the ocean. The ocean of your blissful Self became at once for me a state of everlasting bliss, for me to be and see. I know now that you are me, and you are we, and when I look around some more I will always come back to thee.

Karma Yoga
SEARCHING
Searching means to explore both with your heart and mind the many ways

available in the world to find a connection with the Divine. Searching begins when the desires you have fulfilled are no longer giving you a feeling of satisfaction. And you feel an emptiness and meaninglessness in yourself. Once the emptiness or loneliness is felt inside, you will intuitively seek refuge in more fulfilling activities, until you find an activity that stops the loneliness and gives you a sense of wholeness. Only when you have found what you are looking for will you begin to slow down the search for something else, until eventually you have made a strong commitment to your path, and dig a deep hole in the consciousness of this path consistently.

Questions
1.What are the three worlds?
2.Can you find God in the three worlds?
3.How does it feel to look for God?
4.Where do you look for God?
5.How does it feel to feel that you have found God?
6.What does it mean that God is in the more?
7.Where is the shore of life and how do you go beyond it?
8.What is abundant love?
9.Where is the ocean of your blissful Self?
10.Why is it important to cry and let go of your tears?

Today: Remember always that whenever you get lost or cannot find your Self that as long as you keep looking you will find your way back to the blissful Self.

Verse 8

Verse
'The Lord supports this universe which consists of a combination of the perishable and the imperishable, the manifest and the unmanifest, as long as the Individual Soul does not know the Lord, he is attached to the sensual pleasures. He becomes the enjoyer and is bound. When he knows the Lord, he is released from all fetters.'

JnaniYoga
After exploring the Divine, and what Divinity actually means to you, you must explore its opposite. It is impossible to actually know something is real without first truly experiencing its opposite, what it is not. Now is the time to study from an objective perspective the material world surrounding you. There is so much material to choose from in the west. Mostly, people are completely merged with

·Chapter I·

their material reality and are unable to separate themselves from it. Now is the time to practice seeing your material world from a perspective of distance and separation, watching it work and unfold.

Bhakti Yoga
You cannot destroy me, I am indestructible. I am not of this world of matter and material, I am not of any world attached to this. Know this, that I am not of any world, I am not of any form, I am the formless experiencer of the world. The world is an experience of matter to me, I cannot visualise anything or attribute anything real to me.

Karma Yoga
REALISATIONS
Realisations are tiny droplets of Divine Consciousness. To realise something means to know that thing is real, that it is the Truth. When one realises a 'new' Truth into their own Individual Consciousness, it creates a feeling of connection, oneness, love and a deep sense of awe towards God. God is moving you forwards towards the reality of who you are, and this makes you feel closer to him, and more aware of who he truly is. Realisations cannot be forced into your awareness, they cannot be controlled. You cannot make yourself know something. You have to push through all your desires, attachments and egotistical behaviours. And then, only when you face your inner demons will God enlighten you to your True Nature. This enlightenment occurs naturally when you display faith and courage in accepting you have failings and imperfections, but are still trying to believe that you are worthy of a relationship with God and your True Self.

Questions
1.What cannot be destroyed?
2.How are you indestructable?
3.What is the world of matter?
4.Describe the material world and the difference between it and the spiritual world.
5.What world do you originate from?
6.Are you attached to this material world?
7.How do you see your form?
8.What is the formless experiencer of the world?
9.What does it mean to 'experience' matter?
10.Can you imagine seeing everything is unreal, what would this be like?

Today: Feel all forms of matter and material as separate from you, including your body, your mind and your senses. Hold your awareness of that part of you and observe how no matter what you do, you cannot destroy it.

·Chapter I·

Verse 9

Verse
'The knowing Lord and the unknowing individual soul, the omnipotent and impotent, are both unborn. She (nature, prakriti) too, who is connected with the enjoyer and objects of enjoyment, who causes the realisation of the enjoyer and the enjoyed is unborn. When all these three are realised as Brahman, the Self becomes infinite, universal and inactive.'

JnaniYoga
Surrender is necessary now, surrender to a power greater than yourself. In surrendering you face the ultimate truth of being alone, and that no one can help you on your journey but the unknown entity which is God. You have to face all your inner demons, your manipulations, your lies, your behaviours that lead you towards the illusion of connection with another. There are no real connections on this plane of existence. Everyone here is alone, and journeying through unknown territory without a guidebook or map. You can look to others, but they cannot show you the way. The way for them is not the way for you. Your journey may look and feel the same as another, but no one has the same unique karma that you have reincarnated into, no one has to face the territory that you must venture into. And for this reason alone, you must rely on a power greater than yourself to guide you, to hold your hand, to carry you when you feel weak. This power greater than you, this force for good, for truth, for love, can only be found in God. And to realise God's True Nature, you must surrender your will, your desires and let go of all results and attachments to a desired outcome of your own making.

Bhakti Yoga
Manifestation, power, creation, Shakti. All are part of an unknown experience by the Atman. The Atman knows not what the experience is that has come into being until that experience is made manifest in its entirety, in its full creative force within the Self.

What is it to manifest in fullness and greatness? The power of the mighty Shakti awakening that nature of the Atman to itself. How do I know this? How do I know this is real? The confusion, the doubt, the weaknesses, the delicacies of my experience. How will I know the manifest is real? I need to know, to be fed with the experience of knowledge, of truth, to know that I am in the experience of myself, without doubt, without fear. I need you to help me, to show me to myself, my Atman, to cling, to hold, to grasp, to grab, to not let go, to hold on so tightly it hurts so much. To surrender, to know. To surrender is to know, to know is to surrender. The manifestation of my nature is to let go, to know my Atman is to let

·Chapter I·

go. To not feel a part of the experience of myself but feel aware of it, to observe it, to witness. The witness experiences the Atman to let it go.

Karma Yoga
SURRENDER
Surrender is to completely fold yourself into a foetus like shape and allow the Divine Creator to welcome you into his womb. It is to be like a needy baby, seeking food and comfort only from God. It is to let go of all attachments to worldly needs, and recognise the only need you have is for God's love.
Surrendering feels like you are throwing away everything you have known to be real for you, and laying yourself down at God's feet, and humbly asking for God's will to be done, not your own.

Questions
1.What is Shakti?
2.How does Shakti awaken you to your Atman's nature?
3.How does manifestation occur in your being?
4.How do you know that something has manifested?
5.When do you know something is real?
6.What is knowledge and truth?
7.How can you face your doubts and fears?
8.What do you do to practice the art of surrendering in your life?
9.Have you ever experienced your Atman, and how it really feels to let go?
10.What does it mean to witness your self?

Today: Practice letting go of anything you feel attached to in any given moment. In the moment of letting go witness your Atman as it holds onto nothing - nothing at all.

Verse 10

Verse
'Matter is perishable, but God (Hara) is immortal and imperishable. He, the only God, rules over the perishable matter and the Individual Souls. By meditating upon Him, by union with Him and by becoming one with Him, there is finally cessation of all illusion.'

JnaniYoga
It is time to experience a greater depth of your Self, it is time to journey even deeper still into an awareness of yourself. It is time to let go of the past and all you have clung to, and time to find a Guru - a guide, a teacher, a knower of Brahman.

·Chapter I·

Only with an accomplished teacher can you ever imagine feeling safe enough to go deeper into your Self. It is a fearful, challenging journey you are on, with many obstacles. And to truly make the journey you must reach out and ask for assistance. Guidance out of the darkness and towards the light. Your heart will pull you towards many teachers, but you must feel a connection that could not be experienced anywhere else for you to be sincerely open to their direction and more, importantly, Love. They will take you places that you never thought could be possible. It will be an awe inspiring journey, and worth every moment.

Bhakti Yoga
It matters not what we bring into this world with us, it matters what we take away with us. It counts, the blessings, the awarenesses, the insights, the knowledge, the love, the karmic releases, all count to our final summation. When we leave this existence to merge blissfully into the next we must consider what we take away with us. All our days, our moments , our weeks, our months, our years, all must be spent in remembrance of the Lord, the Supreme Lord who sent us here to do our duty. How we must never forget our mission, our reason for manifesting was, and always will be to become one with Him again.

Karma Yoga
DEVOTION
Devotion is love, absolute love towards another. It is complete self abandonment, whereby in the act of devotion you can completely let go and serve the needs of God through another. Whether it be an individual Guru or an established, organisation , such as religion, you must find an object for you to practice the art of devotion. Once found, you must immerse yourself in this love and cultivate an inner and outer relationship until you can trust and let go enough to receive love. The receiving of love from God through this vehicle is immeasurable. There is no other experience that can be compared to it. It can take you to places inside yourself that you did not even imagine existed. It can enable you to do things that you would not think possible.

Questions
1.What do we bring into this world?
2.What would you want to take out of this world with you?
3.Why do blessings, awarenesses, insights and knowledge count?
4.What are karmic releases?
5.What is the final summation?
6.Do you consider what you take into your next existence?
7.How do you spend time in remembrance of the Lord?
8.Who is the Supreme Lord who has sent you here to do your duty?

·Chapter I·

9.What does your personal mission look like?
10.Who do you desire to become one with again?

Today: Quiet the mind and allow awareness to merge with every drop of blissful consciousness.

Verse 11

Verse
'By knowledge of God all the bonds (of ignorance) are destroyed; there is cessation of birth and death with distress destroyed. By meditating on him one attains the third state, universal lordship at the dissolution of the body. All his desires are gratified and he becomes one without a second.'

JnaniYoga
Now it is time to speak with God, to build an everlasting relationship with God. People see God as an unknown entity far from their reach, and therefore do not realise that to realise their true nature they must spend time with God. If you wanted to learn about God, and how to build a relationship with him, you would ask someone who has a relationship with God, and who can show you how to practice these skills yourself. It is likened to one who has a successful relationship with their spouse, parent, child etc. You would ask them how, you would observe their example. This is the same with a Guru. A Guru is an example of how to build a relationship with God to reach enlightenment. The Guru does not even have to speak, or share any of the how. But, you must observe and witness the way in which they act and behave. Trusting at all times that the Guru you have chosen to observe is fully capable of leading you closer to God purely by example. It is this trust in the Guru that must now be nurtured within and without.

Bhakti Yoga
I am not worthy of your loving, tender care. I am not valued at all. I am not of this world and therefore cannot exist one more moment without your Grace. My Grace is full of life and worth and adequacy. I cannot exist for you alone anymore, I cannot exist at all. I am afraid of leaving you and not knowing you, I am afraid of loving you and not having you. I don't want to share a moment of sadness, of pain, anymore. Please I beg of you release me from the bondage of self enquiry, release me from the shackles of self ignorance. I cannot bear to be without you a moment longer. I have nowhere to go but with you, I have nowhere to be but with you, I have nowhere that truly feels real but when I am by your side. Direct me to a version of the Self that is free from bondage, free from pain, the suffering in my heart.

·Chapter I·

I can no longer bear these vultures of discontent, of forbearance, of disillusionment, I can no longer tolerate with or without you. I need you to set me free, I need you to release me. I am a slave to you. I am a slave to me. I am a slave to thee. Release me, oh Brahman. Free me, oh Brahman. I am yours. I am yours.

Karma Yoga GRACE

Grace is the favour of the Guru towards you. A Guru, or knower of Brahman, will observe your behaviour, both inner and outer, towards God through him or her. And, it is from this observation that they will determine your worthiness. The more a Guru deems you worthy, the more they will grant you boons. These boons will enlighten you, and bring you ever closer to God. There is nothing on earth that can compare to the power and the glory of this Grace. Words can never fully describe the enormous gifts that can be showered on the Guru's devoted disciples. Grace comes to you when you least expect it, but it is earned from actions, feelings and thoughts selflessly given to God each day of your life. Grace brings hope, love, knowledge, faith and can save you from so much unnecessary suffering in your life.

Questions

1.What does it mean to be worthy?
2.Do you value yourself, and if so how?
3.What is Grace?
4.Are you afraid of never knowing God?
5.How does Self enquiry make you feel?
6.Do you feel driven to let go of your Self ignorance?
7.Describe the experience of being without God?
8.What is it like to be by God's side?
9.What is discontentment, forbearance and disillusionment?
10.How does Brahman release you and set you free?

Today: Free yourself for a moment from anything in your life that holds you back from experiencing your one True Self. Anything that makes you feel overwhelming sadness to be away from your only love.

Verse 12

Verse

'This is to be known as eternally existing in one's own Self. Truly there is nothing higher than that to be known. When one recognises the enjoyer,

·Chapter I·

the object of enjoyment and the dispenser or the Supreme Ruler, all has been said. This is the threefold Brahman.'

JnaniYoga
The Self is now aligned with its true calling, to serve God tirelessly, to know thyself, and to love yourself unconditionally. Once experienced, even for just one moment, the Self, and your awareness of it is breathtaking and awe inspiring. All your hard work, pushing yourself towards an even greater awareness of who you are starts to pay off. You feel alive, free and full of wonderment for who you really are. You begin to show signs of enlightenment. Your mind is cleare,r your feelings more refined, your actions more selfless and devoted to the Divine. Physical life begins to change. Choices and decisions become easier, worries that once felt so real lose their grip upon your mind . A fresh outlook and perception of you, the world and your environment blossoms . The energy and zeal required to carry on towards Self Realisation is realised within, and strength and courage manifest inside to keep you going .

Bhakti Yoga
I am everything to me, I am free, there is nothing I require, desire or need. I am in love with the need only for the Self. The Self is all I have ever dreamed of, all I have ever wanted. I want for nothing and I need nothing other than you. You I have at all times now. I hold you in my arms of unconditionality and I know of nothing else existing but us. We are together now free, we are holding each other in the warmth of our Self, the Self we were intended to exist with. There was no other purpose than this. Nothing else exists but this. I cannot imagine I could ever falter from this One Truth. The Ultimate Truth that you brought me here to see, that I am you and you are indeed me. One without a second. No other than that. No other than that. No other than that.

Karma Yoga
THE SELF
The Self is pure awakened blissful consciousness. It is the awareness of the Divine in your being. An energy of love flows more consistently through you. Strength and wisdom become a normal existence for you. The perception of your mind is clear and crisp. Your emotions are more childlike, and no longer grip your concentration like they once did . Your vision repairs, and you see everyone and everything through the eyes of God. Your relationships change to a more honest reflection of who you really are. Life is worth living once again. Freedom is achievable. Hope springs from your heart. You are now experiencing more and more of the Truth. God is love, you are love. Love is all you need or want.

·Chapter I·

Questions
1.What does it mean to be everything to yourself?
2.Are you free?
3.Do you require, desire or need anything other than God?
4.Are you in love with your Self?
5.What is unconditionality?
6.Describe the warmth of your Self.
7.Is it your purpose to realise the Self?
8.What is the 'One' Truth?
9.How do you experience the Ultimate Truth?
10.What does it mean to be one without a second?

Today: I am free. Tell yourself, 'I am free. There is nothing to get, or want or need. I am already free. I was a/ways free and I am always free. '

Verse 13

Verse
'As fire is not perceived when it is latent in its cause, the firewood, and yet there is no destruction of its subtle form, because it is again perceived in its cause the firewood by rubbing, so also the Atman is perceived in the body by meditating on the sacred syllable Orn.'

JnaniYoga
A fear infiltrates your blissful self. It weaves through all your hard work, and relentlessly attempts to destroy your belief in who you are, and what you have become. Your mind chatters endlessly, hour upon hour, minute upon minute. Restless and agitated. It drives you towards the fear, and the voice inside your mind that speaks of nothing real. The transient voices of self hatred, disbelief and uncertainty. Can I become Self Realised? Do I have what it takes? Will I succeed? How it is possible when I think this, feel that, do the unthinkable acts? And, you wane, you give in, you surrender to its impermanence. And then, as if from nowhere another voice speaks to you. A soft, gentle, loving voice beckons you away from the darkness of this egoic trip and requests that you believe, that you trust, that you continue on your path. That you recommit to your spiritual practices, that you push yourself even harder onwards and upwards towards God.

·Chapter I·

Bhakti Yoga

My body cannot give me the experience I am searching for. I am expecting the impossible from the unreal. I am losing sight of my Truth, the Truth you sent me here to know, that only an experience of Self can connect me to the source, to you. Oh Brahman, my body is not I, it is not you. It is not free, it is tied to a reality far from me, one of pain, misery and untold suffering. I cannot realise myself from this bondage of body identification without death. I must follow my heart and go beyond my body and its limitations. I must experience my source. I must identify myself to my subtle form, the energy of my being is lucid and free. It does not crave, or desire; it is wholeness and complete. I can alleviate my suffering inside myself only when I journey inside to hear the voice of my Self as it cries out your name, cries out to you, 'Orn'. The vibration of Orn leaves me and in its place I find you. There in the beingness of my Self. Still, aware, alone, unattached, connected absolutely to the source of all. I hear you, I say, oh Brahman, I hear you.

Karma Yoga

FAITH

Faith is the ability to face your fears, doubts and uncertainties head on. It is the unwavering belief that what you are doing is right, and that no harm can ever come to you. Faith keeps you going, it transforms a relentless barrage of abuse from your mind to a focused , single minded determination towards Truth. It reminds you of the light, and awakens you to the lies that the darkness showers upon you daily. It turns your awareness away from deceit and grounds in your reality. The reality that you are one with God, and your only need is to come closer and closer to him. Your heart feels stronger, and more dedicated to Truth.

Questions

1.How do you expect the impossible from the unreal?
2.How do you lose sight of the Truth?
3.Have you experienced your Self and how it connects you to the source?
4.How is your body not who you are?
5.Describe body identification.
6.How do you connect to your source?
7.How do you identify with your subtle form?
8.Do you listen to the voice of your Self as it cries out to God?
9.Describe the beingness of your Self.
10.What is it like when you actually hear God inside?

Today: After practicing 'Om', hear the sound of your Self as it connects to the source of All.

·Chapter I·

Verse 14

Verse
'By making one's own body the lower piece of wood or friction stick, and the syllable Orn the upper friction stick and by practicing the friction or churning of meditation, one will realise God who is hidden, as it were.'

JnaniYoga
The journey of separating from your ego, and building a relationship with your True Self is, of course, a challenge. And at times feels confusing and complex. The constant rollercoaster ride of going between the ego and the Self can feel upsetting and exhausting - it can feel sometimes like it's not actually worth the pain. But, when you remember, the pain of being constantly unconscious and unaware of your True Nature is far greater than the journey of remembering. Nothing can compare to the experience of even just moments of Truth, Love and Knowledg e. Even the pain of forgetting is not as harsh, or as heavy as the pain of never remembering. You must carry on, you must muster up all your strength and resources. You must not give in to the voice inside that tells you that you cannot succeed. You need now to believe in yourself, and your ability to manifest the real reason for your existence, right now in this precious moment.

Bhakti Yoga
Oh Brahman, oh yes I have found you hidden within my being, hidden within my own material being. You are here with me all the time, alone am I not anymore. I am with you inside my whole being, my whole being reverberates with the sound of you. You are with me when the darkness of ignorance falls upon my material existence. You are with me when the illusion of separate existence pulls and tears me apart from everything you have shown me to be real. I am apart no more, I am apart no more. My being sings out in glory of your magnificence that all along in my misery to realise you were always there and never was I alone. I can no longer deny your love for me, I can no longer deny my love for thee.

Karma Yoga
BELIEF
There are two types of belief - the belief in yourself, and the belief in God. It is possible and necessary to separate these two ideas from each other. The ego tells you to believe that you are not separate from God, that everything that you are is the result, the fault of God. This is a lie. And when you can recognise this deceit, you can recognise that your belief in yourself is tainted by your defects of character and realise that actually separating yourself and your ego helps you tenfold to develop a relationship with both your true self and God. Letting your

·Chapter I·

ego be what it has become, and seeing a more honest version of yourself makes all the difference now between success and failure. If you can see the separation at this point you can choose, and it is this ability to choose that enables you to succeed. Because as you see this separation inside, you also realise that God does not have an ego, and that the Self you are experiencing is magnificent but only a mere fragment of what God actually is and is capable of. This realisation strengthens your belief in God, and makes you feel that anything is possible. This is belief. Realising that God is capable of anything, and that the part of you that is God is also capable of anything.

Questions
1.What is your material being?
2.How can you find Brahman hidden within your own being?
3.What does it feel like to know that Brahman is with you all the time?
4.How does it feel to know that you are not alone?
5.Describe how your whole being reverberates with the sound of Brahman.
6.How does the illusion of separate existence pull and tear you apart from Brahman?
7.What have you been shown to be real?
8.How do you sing out in glory of your magnificence?
9.Describe how you can no longer deny God's love for you.
10.How do you love your Self?

Today: Realise whenever you feel alone that you are with me. I am always by your side.

Verse 15

Verse
'As oil in sesame seeds, as butter in curd, as water in river beds, and as fire in wood, even so is Atman perceived within his own self by a person who beholds him by truth and austerity.'

JnaniYoga
All you can see, feel and think of is of God. You are experiencing oneness now more and more. You feel connected to everything that is, and ever was. Love permeates your being now, and your consciousness is elevated to greater heights. Your perception of the world and your environment is changing. You see yourself in all, and the reflections from your outer world are shifting to a more honest, open manifestation of the Divine.

·Chapter I·

Bhakti Yoga
I know now that nothing exists but you. I need no one, or nothing, everything I realised into my existence I set free, to journey on its own without me. I can feel you now and nothing I need is not with you. I am separate no more from you, I am so close to you that you cannot see the space between us, it has vanished so easily because the space was never real. I see that now, but I know that now.
I know you, oh Brahman, I know you.

Karma
SINGLE MINDEDNESS
Single mindedness is when all you can think, feel and do is for God. The ego no longer grips hold of you tightly, its reign of fear over you has subsided. And, all you want is to merge back soon into a blissful state of consciousness. You are driven by a need far greater than any physical need, a need for Love. The Love that transports you to a state of being that folds your mind into your heart once more. And you can remember daily your goal, your desire, your lust for oneness with God.

Questions
1.What does it mean to know?
2.What does it feel like to need no one, or nothing, but God?
3.What have you realised into existence thus far?
4.How do your realisations journey on their own?
5.Can you feel your oneness with God?
6.Can you see the space between you and God?
7.Are you separate from God really in Truth?
8.How is the space between you and God not real? 9. Describe what you know.
10.Discuss/share your relationship with Brahman when you are single minded and focused .

Today: Feel the Atman inside your being. Try to separate yourself from it, and realise it cannot be done.

Verse 16

Verse
'The Atman which pervades all things like butter in milk is rooted in Self knowledge and austerity. This is the mystic doctrine (Upanishad) concerning Brahman.

·Chapter I·

JnaniYoga
Oneness is like sitting in God's home in front of a warm fire, safe and comforted. It is this feeling generated inside your being that you can experience at any given moment that drives you forward. Just one experience in your life of this safety can move mountains, regions, terrains of unrealised consciousness inside. You are that, you are Divine Consciousness, unrealised but yet to be realised. There is a light, a warmth in you, that is guiding you now, directing you. Nothing can switch off this light of Divinity, even unconsciousness cannot turn it off. It will always be yours to return to whenever you remember.

Bhakti Yoga
Reading this verse is like looking directly into the eyes of mine that we both created together for our own good. I came here to see you for real, that you are me and exist only for you. But therefore for me. Everything I do, everything I see, everything I feel, everything I think, is us. We are so interconnected that we cannot separate. I am like the oil placed in the water of your Divine ocean. Once I join you I merge and even though it feels like a sheath of me lays on top of you unable to merge completely, I see now that that is also you, that is also me, free to experience myself as you, connected to you, at one with you. But still myself. Still able to identify with my own consciousness. What beauty is your Grace that you would allow me the amazing opportunity to be connected with you, not separate but still able to see, to feel, to know, to think of us together. How could I have been so ignorant to not know this before? How could I have felt alone when we were always together? Shiva and Shakti dancing, embracing our differences but aware always of our sameness, our oneness, and complete interconnectedness. My Jiva and you. Oh Brahman, I have so missed us and our dance, please always hold my hand in yours, please always bring my hips close to yours and may we forever dance the cosmic dance, the music of oneness forever in our hearts.

Karma Yoga
ONENESS
Oneness is the realisation that you are God. You are Divine, and no matter what you think, feel or do in the future you will always know that this is the truth of your existence. Full Realisation does not have to occur for you to know now that everything you are doing is taking you ever closer to more of yourself. You cannot fail, even if full Realisation does not manifest in this incarnation, it will, it has to. There is no other reason for existing but this.

Questions
1.Why did you come here?

·Chapter I·

2.What does it feel like to know you exist only for God?
3.What is interconnectedness?
4.Can you describe the Divine ocean of consciousness?
5.What is it like to merge with God?
6.When you are one with God, how do you see yourself?
7.What is your own consciousness like?
8.What is Shiva and Shakti?
9.Describe your Jiva.
10.Describe the dance between Shiva and Shakti.

Today: Dance with God. As you move feel your hands and your hips connected to the source. The source of all that is and all that will ever be - Brahman!

·Chapter I·

Main Point of Chapter I

THE RELATIONSHIP BETWEEN BRAHMAN AND THE SELF

The main point being conveyed to you throughout Chapter I is about your relationship with Brahman from the viewpoint of your 'SELF'. The Self inside all beings must cultivate a deeper, more meaningful relationship with Brahman for Self Realisation to begin. This relationship is the basis of Self Realisation. The foundation upon which an individual being stands on is paramount. This relationship starts with humility, and your need for an open mind.

The process now has its goal, and the steps to realise this goal are as follows:

a)A sense of individuality.
b)Identifying with your Atman.
c)Begin the journey of renunciation.
d)Become more aware of the Ultimate Truth.
e)Realise the real need inside.
f) Tirelessly search for a path.
g)Experience realisations.
h)Develop a capacity of surrender to his will.
i)Cultivate devotion to a power greater than yourself.
j)Receive an abundance of God's grace to assist and support you.
k)Understand the Self as it really is separate from the non-self.
l)Deepen your faith so you may conquer your fears and doubts.
m)Strengthen your belief in yourself and God.
n)Become single minded and focused.
o)Experience more and more moments of oneness.

This chapter outlines and clearly guides you towards an ever greater experience of how to build a relationship with Brahman, so it is elevated from a human level relationship to one of the Divine.

·Chapter II·

Verse 1

Verse
'Concentrating first the mind and the senses (upon Brahman) for realising the Truth, may Savitri, having seen the illuminating fire, bring it out of the earth.'

JnaniYoga
It is not the mind itself that is the problem, but the lack of illuminated consciousness within the mind. The mind, of itself, is an empty vessel able to be filled with whatever you choose to place inside. The object, or goal, of Self Realisation is that the mind be filled with love, pure Divine Consciousness. An individual who is not yet fully realised will have a mind full of sensory, active consciousness. This active consciousness is necessary for the searching needed to find out the Truth. The perfect searching mind is one that is in a cycle of activity, love, activity. To develop an awareness of this cycle further, it is a requirement of searching for the Truth that you are able to generate activity in the mind that can look, think, discern etc. But, it is also necessary that on reaching a particular truth, you are able to be with that truth in an energy of love.

Bhakti Yoga
I am not the body and I am not the mind. My mind is in me, and yet my mind is free. I am not faithful to my mind, and yet my mind is faithful to me. I am not the

·Chapter II·

mind, I am not the mind. My mind is illuminated consciousness once it is free, my mind is bondaged, shackled to the tenets of the three worlds and therefore cannot exist for me. I cannot exist with thee, I am not a part of you, and you are not a part of me. I cannot exist for thee. You must exist for me, you must serve me. You must generate as much light as possible, it must burn through your denial, through your doubts and fears. It must tear away at the very fabric of your self-depreciating beliefs. It must rip open the thoughts and ideas to know with all certainty it is bondaged, tied, attached to me.

Karma Yoga
CONSCIOUSNESS
Consciousness is everything to me, I am consciousness. It is the most beautiful form of God that could ever have been realised into being. Everything in existence is consciousness. God created everything in the world from his own consciousness. So therefore, everything in existence is God. When you realise your True Nature and know who you are, you will be able to experience God in everything. You will know that nothing existing is not God. The first verse of Chapter II is enlightening you to this reality. That everything is consciousness. Consciousness is alive, its heart beats, it is a beingness full of love and awareness. It is who you are, your True Nature. Try to see past the form of all things and witness the aspect of everything that is 'alive'.

Questions
1.What are you if you are not the body or the mind?
2.How can your mind be in you, and also free?
3.How are you not faithful to your mind?
4.Explain: 'Your mind is illuminated consciousness.'
5.How is your mind shackled to the tenets of the three worlds?
6.How can your mind serve you?
7.How do you generate light in your mind?
8.How does this light burn away through your denial, doubts and fears?
9.What are your self-depreciating beliefs?
10.How do you rip open your thoughts and ideas and see God inside them?

Today: Listen to scriptures and feel the light of knowledge burn away all your mistaken ideas and beliefs.

Verse 2

Verse
'By the grace of the divine Savitri let us, with concentrated mind, strive

·Chapter II·

vigorously for the attainment of Supreme Bliss.'

JnaniYoga
This pure Divine Consciousness is inside you and everything else in existence, from an ant to a mountain. It is the consciousness of God that connects everything together as one whole entity. Only the lower mind separates and compartmentalises. This lower mind is full of karma, and void of Divine Consciousness. You have to begin to see that the Divine Consciousness can become anything, even your very own Self. It is the perception you have of yourself that needs to change. You will have to work hard to see past your lower mind, and concentrate on the Divine so it can be seen in all its glory within your own mind. Divine Consciousness and your lower mind need to be connected and not separate, and for this to happen you must concentrate.

Bhakti Yoga
I cannot know you by another name. I cannot understand your nature if I do not understand my own. I think we are separate, and in my illusionary mind I search for you outside of myself, I look away from me to find you. And, yet if I was to take the time to know myself, in all certainty I think I would know you. To know you is to know me. I must look to me, at all times . My gaze must wander inside my own mind. I must go deep, deeper and deeper inside my own mind and find the connection between us both. Once that connection is realised I can know you, and to know you is to know.

Karma Yoga
CONNECTION
Connection is an experience of togethe rness, unity. All things are in harmony with one another, even things deemed to be bad, or painful. To experience connection one must see past the separation and realise the Divine in all things . It is the Divine that is able to connect. Only the Divine can generate enough energy to form a perception of connectivity.

Questions
1.What other names do you use to try to know God?
2.What is God's True Nature?
3.What is your own True Nature?
4.Are we separate from God?
5.What is your illusory mind?
6.How do you search for God outside of yourself?
7.How do you get to know yourself?
8.Have you ever gazed inside your own mind?

·Chapter II·

9.Have you experienced a connection between you and God inside your own mind?
10.What is it like when you realise the connection?

Today: Don't look for what God is outside of your Self. Journey inside your own mind and find what connects your mind to God's.

Verse 3

Verse

'Having controlled the senses through which heaven is attained with the mind and the intellect, let Savitri cause them to manifest the divine infinite light.'

JnaniYoga

Experience this depth of reality like no other when you go into an altered state of awareness as you keep your mind focused on one true place within, and free yourself from the sensory input once seemingly in control of what you do, think and feel. Allow all that was once real to you to melt away into the nothingness from whence it came and stay for a while in this place of absolute calm, absolute stillness inside. Close your eyes now, and keep them closed. Close your ears, nose and mouth. And only be in an awareness of your breath. Allow your breath to take you deeper and deeper inside yourself, past the sensory input to a place of nothingness. Keep your consciousness resting in this nothingness for as long as you can. This place that you will journey to within will alleviate so much suffering in this moment, in past moments and ultimately in future moments. It will transform your sensory input, and reduce its effects.

Bhakti Yoga

As I go deeper and deeper inside my own mind I find a place there, a place of stillness and peace where I can realise myself as separate from my external reality. The stimulus from my sensory experiences has vanished without a trace, as if almost the reality of that world was never real at all. I can experience a calm like I have never experienced before. It washes over my consciousness and brings a bliss of knowledge I have not experienced before. This is the light of Divine Consciousness that I have been searching for. I have searched so long now, and so hard. I am so tired that if it is your will I will rest here awhile longer, I will rest here awhile. And all the while whilst I rest here I will think of us, an interconnected place inside me has just woken up. My consciousness feels awake and alive. I think I know what I am here to do. I am here to merge, to let go of all that is outside that once felt so real.

·Chapter II·

And finally become one without a second - one without a second that is you.

Karma Yoga
MEDITATION
Meditation is an art form. It is the ability to draw your consciousness into itself to a whole, a one pointed elevated awareness. Meditation, to be done successfully, must be practiced daily. It must be practiced in a clean environment with no distractions. The goal of meditation is to not open your eyes. This act of closing the eyes draws all activity in the mind to a single point, usually the breath. The breath being an aspect of Brahman, in its more pure form, can act like a catalyst to your Self and awaken you to Truths from a higher realm. As the outer eyes close, the inner eye opens.

Questions
1.What does it mean to go deeper and deeper inside your own mind?
2.Have you ever experienced a place of stillness and peace inside your mind?
3.Can you imagine realising yourself as separate from your external reality?
4.What is the stimulus from your sensory experiences?
5.Is the reality of the world real?
6.Can you describe the bliss of knowledge?
7.What is the light of Divine Consciousness?
8.How are you searching?
9.Has your consciousness awoken to itself as being alive and awake?
10.What does it mean: 'One without a second.'

Today: Meditate, concentrating your awareness inside your mind. Let go of your sensory experiences and journey deeper than you have before.

Verse 4

Verse
'Great is the glory of Savitri who is all-pervading, infinite, all-knowing, the one alone who knows the rules, has arranged the sacrificial rites by the Brahmanas. The wise control their mind and intellect and practice meditation.'

JnaniYoga
Awareness is the realisation that bliss exists, in every second, in every moment it is possible to experience. There are so many other realities that one experiences

·Chapter II·

in the mind, but none that come close to the sheer power of bliss. Bliss is the energy of love, it emanates from love. When one meditates, bliss is being called up from the heart (the Sel and flows up into the mind. This bliss creates a new state of absolute space within the mind, and from this state realisations of Truth can occur effortlessly. Old desires, sensory information, attachments, thoughts, beliefs - all are washed away, cleared, cleaned by the powerful energy of bliss. The object of each individual is to believe in the possibility of bliss, and therefore the reality of awareness can transform a full mind to one of nothingness.

Bhakti Yoga

The light of the sun's rays blind me. They enable me to see, and yet still I cannot see me. The me that is you, I mean. It is blocked from my viewpoint. Help, I cannot see. I want to see all the beauty in the world that you have described to me. In the darkness of my ignorance I fail to see you with thine eyes that you have gracefully given freely to me. I want to see the sunlight as it shines upon the shore of infinite possibilities, of grace, I cannot see what is right there before me. Let me see with thine eyes the coming of the Lord. I desire with all my being, with all that I am, to see you standing there for me in all your glory.The days seem longer and the nights are lighter now. I can see, I can see what you destined me to see. I see you, you are truly magnificent. There is no story I tell, or song to sing, that cannot be undone by you for me. You rightly deserve to know that I am near you now. I can see, I can see. There are no spaces, no gaps, the light shines through it all. My unconscious desires, latent and free, are merged into your awareness. We are together now and we can see that we were destined all along to be together. The one true insight I have gained, the one true knowledge I have sought, the one true awareness I can know. We are in daylight what we are in night. The darkness of illuminated awareness falls upon me and I can see that nothing at all is real, nothing at all is real.

Karma Yoga
AWARENESS

Awareness is what happens to you when your consciousness reaches into your mind, and pulls out all the old, outdated beliefs. Even for a moment, a minute, an hour, you actually experience a state of 'no thoughts' in your mind, other than the realisation of Truth. This state may not remain for very long, but sometimes it will embed itself into your consciousness (psyche) and become a real part of your path to Self.

Questions

1.What can you not see?
2.How can you see the beauty in the world?

·Chapter II·

3.Describe the darkness of your ignorance.
4.What are your infinite possibilities?
5.Can you see the coming of the Lord?
6.Do you experience spaces, or gaps, inside your mind?
7.How do you experience your unconscious desires?
8.What does it mean that your unconscious desires are merged into your awareness?
9.What are you in daylight that you are in night?
10.How can illuminated awareness be the darkness?

Today: In the daylight and in the night know that the nothingness of your mind is real, and the light of your mind forever turning towards the insights and awareness, the knowledge and wisdom of illuminated consciousness when your mind merges back with mine.

Verse 5

Verse
'I worship you ancient Brahman with reverence. My verses go forth like the suns on their course. May the sons of the immortal listen, even those who inhabit celestial regions.'

JnaniYoga
When you have the humility to lay down your ego for awhile, and surrender at the lotus feet of our beloved Brahman, enormous boons reach your mind from a place you cannot even imagine possible. This place of Supreme Consciousness that resides everywhere at all times, is just waiting patiently for you to tap into its resources, to which there are many, they are infinite in number. Worshipping God transforms your mind effortlessly, it fills your mind with insights, awarenesses, heightened perceptions, choices more in line with your True Nature. This state of mind that is reached through worship can only be obtained when your worship is filled with reverence and respect.

Bhakti Yoga
Oh Brahman I see, I feel, I know. I know you are near me, ever closer your gaze falls upon my soul. My mind is free at last to experience your witness to mine eyes having seen the glory of the coming of the Lord, God, Brahman. I revere you, I bow down my being in absolute surrender to your power and magnificence. Nothing of worth or value may ever cast a shadow of doubt upon my being against your absolute wonderment. The awe you invoke and inspire in my being catches hold of me and leaves me without a breath, without reason.

·Chapter II·

You are of untold beauty and transcend all time and space. To be near you, to have you close to me, I am breathless, words no longer matter to me. I cannot even explain to your children how you came into being. Nothing I know can explain you, I am you and you are me. Together we are Divinity personified, beyond all doubt we fight no more. We surrender our alms to you and ask for your never-ending forgiveness for all of our sins of forgetfulness. We remember you. Our minds are together, we are but one entire being, nothing exists but you, nothing is real but you.

Karma Yoga
REVERENCE
Brahman is to be revered. Reverence to our Supreme Lord Brahman is to give all of yourself, even for a single moment, all of your being, not just parts, but all of you, sends every ounce of love from your heart towards God. There is no love for anything or anyone else. There are no distractions, no desires, no attachments. Just for a single moment which is all that is necessary. Your heart fills with love towards God, and the energy of this love you direct towards the object of your devotion. You allow your being to feel small in comparison to this magnificent being, and when this occurs you are in a state of reverence.

Questions
1.What does it feel like when you feel God's gaze upon your soul?
2.What is it like when you witness the glory of God?
3.How do you revere God?
4.How do you surrender to his power and magnificence?
5.How does God invoke and inspire awe in your being?
6.Can you describe the untold beauty of God?
7.How does God transcend time and space?
8.How did God come into being? Can you explain God?
9.What is Divinity personified?
10.How can you surrender your alms to God?

Today: Practice letting go of all preconceived ideas of God and have absolute abandon for Brahman. Surrender your mistaken ideas and beliefs and just revere, spend time enjoying what it feels like to just revere!

Verse 6

Verse
'Where fire is kindled or churned out, where air is controlled, where the soma juice overflows, there the mind is born.'

·Chapter II·

JnaniYoga
At this point in your spiritual practice it is advisable to have some kind of devotional practice, a part of your daily life. A shrine in your home to your chosen God/Guru is most effective. And then, the practice of devotion, worshipping the shrine with as much energy as possible. It is necessary to put much thought, feeling and action into this aspect of your spiritual life, in recognition of your complete surrender to the Supreme Consciousness that assists and supports you daily with your journey of Self Realisation. Worship is paramount, as it is worship that will develop your relationship with God, and your Bhakti.

Bhakti Yoga
Rituals, fire, sacrifices, I want to worship you with self abandon. I want to throw myself down upon your graceful heavens, I will for all the celestial beings to flow into my being and to have mercy on my soul. May my worship be in honour of your absolute Grace that has bestowed me with Realisation. I want you, I really want you. I need you, I really need you. I cannot possibly ever live without you. To live is to be close to you, anything else would be death to me. I would die, my organs would fail me if I could not feel you near me. Everything in my being would stop, it would cease to exist with the very thought of not being with you. Now I have found you, I cannot ever live without you. I need you to breathe, to move, to sigh, to exist. Existence doesn't exist without you.

KarmaYoga
WORSHIP
What is worship? Worship is loving God with complete self abandon. In the act of worship there is no 'I', no you. The 'I' that you identify yourself to be becomes a tiny speck of consciousness, and the egoic 'I' disappears without a trace. This worshipping is the foundation of all spiritual practices, especially if you are without a Guru, or any formal guidance. If there is no worship, the ego self will become credible in its delivery of untruths, such as convincing oneself that you are being spiritual when really you are feeding an ego's sense of bigness, instead of cultivating a relationship with God, and allowing God to expand your 'I' consciousness to that of an Atman, Soul.

Questions
1.What are rituals?
2.How can rituals benefit your spiritual practice?
3.What does it mean: 'Self abandon'?
4.What are the graceful heavens you seek?
5.How does God have mercy on your soul?
6.Does God bestow you with realisations?

·Chapter II·

7.Does worship make you want and need God more?
8.Does it feel like being without God is worse than death?
9.Do you feel like you could not ever live without God?
10.What does it mean: 'Existence doesn't exist without you'?

Today: Write down all the activities you perform in your week and imagine that all are performed with God. Imagine that nothing you will ever do again will be done without God by your side.

Verse 7

Verse
'Let us love the ancient Brahman by the grace of Savitri. If there thou attainest thy source (Brahman) thy former work will no longer bind thee.'

JnaniYoga
There are so many daily activities that will undoubtedly pull you away from your True Nature. It is a great challenge to live in this western world, and its material status. But, you must push yourself with all your might to pull away from the activity that takes you away from your Self. There is a need, a real need, to find a balance between the material and the spiritual, but there is also a need to recognise that some things are just not supporting you in either worlds. The need for an experience of Blissful Consciousness far outweighs the mindfulness that is generated by doing things you know you just shouldn't do. You have to let go of control and allow your nature to show you the way. You must not hold on to the past, and how you used to do things, but allow for change. Change is necessary.

Bhakti Yoga
I cannot feel the grip upon my soul anymore, it has left me for the last time. All the times I have spent remembering and forgetting have gone. I will never forget you again. Oh, what a reality we have created together for ourselves. That nothing else other than us can exist forevermore. What will I do without the ties that bound me to an endless stream of deathly unconsciousness? I never want to feel, or think again, of the past, present and future. I want, I need, to experience you now in all your glory, the blissful presence that I can experience in my mind as my mind is full of nothing but you. I cannot ever forget, and yet I certainly cannot even remember the ties that bound my soul to the darkness of unillumined consciousness. To be free, to be free, oh Brahman, and yet to be so bound to you. How could I have forgotten your endless Grace, your bountiful face imprinted on the mind of my Self, forever free, forever me, forever thee.

·Chapter II·

Karma Yoga
BLISSFUL
When your whole being from head to toe is full of God's love for you, you can say that you are blissful. The energy of God's love fills your being, and your mind, body and soul are at one with your True Nature. It feels like a light has been lit in your entire being, and nothing else can exist but this. Nothing can compare to this. A state of stillness, of oneness to a consciousness that is powerful beyond measure.

Questions
1.What is the grip that holds so tightly upon your soul?
2.Can you describe the process of remembering and forgetting?
3.What reality have you co-created with God?
4.What ties bind you to unconsciousness?
5.What is the past, present and future?
6.What is the blissful presence?
7.Describe a mind full of nothing but God.
8.What does a bound soul feel like?
9.What is unillumined consciousness?
10.What does it mean: 'Your bountiful face imprinted on the mind of my self'?

Today: Feel the ties no longer binding you to the past, present and future. Only have an awareness of the moment, the precious moment.

Verse 8

Verse

'Keeping his body in a straight posture, holding the chest, neck and head erect, and drawing the senses and the mind into the heart, the wise should cross over the fearful currents (of the world) by means of the raft (or boat) of Brahman.'

JnaniYoga
Meditation is a form of worship. And, to experience this form one must practice meditation as the Rishis of thousands of years ago taught. If meditation is not practiced in this way the benefits will be greatly reduced. So, now it is time to practice your posture. One must practice sitting with crossed legs and a straight spine, likened to sitting into your coccyx. Then, holding the chest, neck and head erect, which can be supported (in practice) by placing a book upon your head, and feeling your torso, neck and head stretching upward towards your crown.

·Chapter II·

This practice is creating a vessel from your form (your body), in which to receive and be filled with God's love. It also allows for any unwanted energy to depart your vessel. If you tried to pour water into a glass that was tilted forwards, or backwards, it would be near impossible for the water to enter the vessel. Likewise, if your body is tilted forward, or backwards, or squashed in any way, it becomes impossible to receive and to give to God.

Bhakti Yoga
I feel the realness, the solidity, the reality of consciousness pulling itself willingly into the realms of your Divine home. My heart it beckons me inwardly, towards my Self. My Self that I remember and will never forget. I feel the absolute enormity of the experience flow out from my heart into the whole of my being. My being is light, it's transcendent, it's aware of nothing and yet aware of everything, the bliss as it streams into my being is overwhelming. The joy, the calm, the love as it radiates throughout me. It cannot be described to you by mere words or thoughts, or feelings. The words I write seem so insignificant compared to the experience of my soul. My soul it beckons me forth on a path not yet conquered, and yet conquer it I must. I must hear my heart, and all the while be transcendent of all that I am, feel and do. Oh, I am home at last, a voyage journeyed with every particle of my being involved, in line, in sync with all that I am. All that I am, I am, I so really, truly am.

Karma Yoga
TRANSCENDENCE
Transcendence, the art of going beyond all that is and reaching a higher place, where all that is becomes all that you are. It is a place beyond your past, present and future, where everything you thought, felt, or imagined yourself to be has flowed away from your Self, and a more accurate, honest account of your Self remains. I think that people imagine that to realise your True Nature you have to focus on all that you are not, and practice letting it go to reach your True Nature. But, this is a lie. To reach your True Nature, one must go beyond, far beyond this mistaken belief. One must not focus on mistaken beliefs, but reach above and beyond their limitations to a place where Truth exists. Transcendence is one's ability to focus only on Truth and not be pulled down by lies and past mistaken beliefs.

Questions
1.How do you practice meditation?
2.What do you think about the Rishis technique of meditation?
3.Can you draw your senses and mind into your heart?

·Chapter II·

4.When you sit in a meditation posture do you trust that your consciousness is pulling itself willingly into your heart, without effort, naturally?
5.Can you hear your heart beckoning you inwardly towards your Self?
6.Can you feel your heart sending love out into your entire being?
7.How is your being light and transcendent?
8.Describe being overwhelmed by bliss.
9.Do you believe it is your heart that beckons you forth on your path?
10.What does it mean to be transcendent of all that you are?

Today: Sit in a meditation posture and draw the consciousness of love into your heart by feeling the nature of Brahman with all your might, every particle of your being!

Verse 9

Verse
'Controlling the senses, repressing and regulating the breathings, checking the movements of the body, gently breathing through the nostrils, the wise should undistractedly restrain his mind, that chariot yoked with vicious horses.'

JnaniYoga
Once you have mastered the art of posture during meditation and you have started to experience your senses and your mind fold into your heart, it is time to take control of the senses, by repressing and regulating the breath, checking the movements of the body, so that they are still, and gently breathing through your nostrils. This will take some time to master, and should not be rushed or taken lightly. One must be serious when practicing this form of worship. It is advisable to separate each stage:

1.Repressing and regulating breathing - by bringing the breathing into the heart space, not too loud or heavy still, shallow breathing in the heart.
2.Checking the movement of the body - sitting absolutely still, not fidgeting and practicing breathing when discomfort arises.
3.Gently breathing through the nostrils - inhaling and exhaling using the nostrils softly and gently, not breathing using the mouth.

All these aspects of meditation should be practiced separately throughout daily life. One, to accustom yourself to their benefit and need, but also to allow for confidence. Attempting this form of meditation in the western world with its myriads of distractions is unadvisable, it is far better to gain confidence in each

·Chapter II·

step first before trying to integrate each step. Once the practice begins to instill confidence then, and only then, must one begin to integrate them and seriously sit in meditation.

Bhakti Yoga

I am not here anymore, I don't exist. The depth and lucidity inside here is transparent. It is warm and tender, soft and malleable. The connection can be felt to all that is real, the reality of this realness is amazing. The 'I' that identified myself is no longer gripping my consciousness to its lower nature. The awareness of my inner being is so strong, and real. When the sensory experiences no longer draw upon my soul to live, to breathe, the 'I' vanishes without any trace of its reality. The manifestation of my Self that takes its place is so quick, it folds my mind into my heart. My whole being resides there, with no other existence, no other external reality but itself. The stillness, the softness, the grace in which it effortlessly transforms my consciousness to its existential Self is enormous and awe inspiring. To be at one with my Creator, to have no awareness other than the one true Supreme Brahman, oh what a reality this is. Not wanting to read, not wanting to write, not wanting to study, eat, think or feel. Just wanting, needing, no having to - without will to rest, to be, to know - that only here in this home that you designed and manufactured for me is everything.

Karma Yoga

BEING

Being is the goal of practicing meditation. It is the ability to sit within one's Self in absolute peace without any sensory input, and just be. The presence of God is experienced inside, and no other activity is generated. There is no other, no second. Only oneness with the Divine. This is when meditation, and Self Realisation becomes more a way of life, rather than something practiced.

Questions

1.Can you control your senses?
2.How do you feel about regulating your breathing, keeping the body movements still, and gently breathing through the nostrils?
3.What does it mean to restrain the mind?
4.Can you imagine the 'I' not existing anymore?
5.How does the 'I' grip you to your lower nature?
6.What do the sensory experiences do when they draw from your soul?
7.What does it feel like when your mind folds into your heart?
8.'You are at one with your creator.' Explain.
9.What is your awareness of the one true Supreme Brahman?
10.What is it like to not want to read, write, study, eat, think or feel?

·Chapter II·

Today: Just sit for a while practicing 'being', without sensory experience. Not meditating, being. And have only an awareness of Brahman and you together inside.

Verse 10

Verse
'One should perform his exercises in concentration on a level place, free from pebbles, fire, wind, dust, dampness and disturbing noises, where the scenery is charming and pleasing to the eyes and where there are bowers, caves, good water - places which help the practice of concentration.'

JnaniYoga
The next stage in the practice of meditation is your environment. It is paramount that your concentration can develop, and is supported by your environment. There should be no disturbing noises, the ground should be level and free from discomfort, and the scenery should be conducive to relaxation. In order to deepen your meditation you will need to create opportunities without distractions. This is recognising that the practice is more important than anything else and must be placed in the highest esteem within your daily life.

Bhakti Yoga
Nothing can distract me from this place I have found within my being, you could move heaven and earth and my being will remain forever at this place of solace and solitude. My being is warm and still, softness and contentment the language it has found to articulate its experience of itself. The warmth feeds my being, the only food I need, the only food I will ever need again. The contentment as it fills my being alludes to a place further still inside my being that I have not reached yet, a place of even smoother, richer, lighter planes. Ones where the darkness of noise and chatter cannot prevail. It cannot stick anymore to the sides of my being, the glue of Divine concentration flowing through now, reaching all the places once forgotten. Now, in my awareness I remember that the stillness exists, and is as real as ever before.

Karma Yoga
CONTENTMENT
A place within where your Self resides, and has no desire for anything other than that place. There is nothing pulling you away from this inner space that has remembered who it is, and why it exists. It is an inner knowing that this is what was intended for you, and all the activity, drama and confusion that lies behind you was just an illusion, a facade hiding your true inner intention from view.

·Chapter II·

Questions

1.What is the inner experience felt when meditation is practiced in the correct environment, as opposed to an incorrect one?
2.Can you describe concentration?
3.What are your distractions?
4.Describe solace and solitude .
5.Do you ever experience contentment?
6.Where does contentment allude to further still?
7.Where are the smoother, richer, lighter planes of existence?
8.Describe the darkness of noise and chatter.
9.How is Divine concentration different from human concentration?
10.Can you describe the stillness experienced whilst in a state of contentment?

Today: Sit quietly in a place without distractions, and connect with the soft, still, warm place within your own being. Stay there awhile concentrating on your breath.

Verse 11

Verse

'When yoga is being performed forms like snow or frost, smoke, the sun, fire, wind, fire-fly, lightning, crystal and the moon appear. They precede the manifestation of Brahman.'

JnaniYoga

The practice of meditation is taking shape and deepening your awareness of Self. And now, you will begin to experience altered states of consciousness within your own mind. An amazing journey has now begun inside your mind that will transform all your outer experiences, your perception of life will change with the changing consciousness. You have to build a relationship with your mind. For this you will need to be open to whatever God decides you are ready to experience. So much can be experienced, but openness to different states of awareness is necessary.

Bhakti Yoga

You must live, and breathe, a constant state of practice now, only true practice can bring you to me now. I am here waiting for you, as I always have been. No longer am I a concept far away from your own reality. My reality is as real to you as it always was, and yet you stayed there for awhile contemplating my existence. Uncertainties, doubts and fears leave you now, and I am ready to take their place. You must feel worthy, you must feel the need, the desire, the lust, the passion for me.

·Chapter II·

This dream you seek must feel possible now, more than ever you must search, you must go to places you never imagined could exist. You must journey deep, low, high, here and there. There must be no corner of your mind left undiscovered. You will find me. When you have exhausted every space in your being, you will find me. There is no place I cannot be for you to realise my nature is your own, it was designed by the same hands, the same mind, the same, we are the same. The heartbeat you feel is my heartbeat. The sound of your breath is my breath. The stillness of your Soul is my Soul. We are one, we are one, we are one.

Karma Yoga
STILLNESS
Imagine consciousness cannot move, it is an immovable object. This is stillness. There are times for consciousness to move, and times for it to stay still. Shiva is still, Shakti is movement. So, therefore stillness is an aspect of Shiva consciousness. A frame of time is frozen, and without movement. Within this frame of frozen time there is an awareness, a glimpse of God. This is meditation. The mind is frozen, all activity ceases and in the moment of stillness God is seen, heard or felt. Stillness is a state within the mind, and has no relationship with physical stillness, and yet mindful stillness does create physical stillness - so in fact it is the inner stillness that creates the outer, and not the other way around.

Questions
1.What does it mean, 'snow, frost, smoke, the sun, wind, fire-fly, lightning, crystal, and the moon appear,' when meditating'?
2.Can you describe experiences that you have had whilst meditating where your mind has appeared like snow, frost, smoke etc?
3.What is the manifestation of Brahman in the mind?
4.What stops, or enables, you to be in a constant state of practice?
5.How do you contemplate God's existence?
6.Do you feel worthy? Do you feel lust, passion and need for God?
7.Does it excite you that you can explore your own mind?
8.'When you have exhausted every space in your being you will find God.' What does this mean?
9.'Your mind and God's mind are the same.' Discuss.
10.'You and God are one.' What experiences do you have that validate this statement?

Today: Start to keep a daily journal to record the state of mind experienced whilst meditating. Record all sounds, colours, textures of your mind, not just your thought state.

·Chapter II·

Verse 12

Verse
'When the fivefold quality of yoga arising from earth, water, fire, air and ether has been produced, then the yogi is endowed with a body made strong by the fire of yoga and so he will not be affected by disease, old age or death.'

JnaniYoga
When your practice is aligned, and all parts are working as an interconnected whole, and your meditation is creating an altered state of awareness within your fabric of life, an experience so vast, so awe inspiring will unfold onto this fabric. An awareness of Brahman and your entire being manifesting as Brahman will occur. 'I am Brahman' will become a normal state of knowing for you, and a heightened state of awareness in relation to your non-Brahman self will be emphasised. Life will open up, and events will take place that you before could only imagine.

Bhakti Yoga
The body, home to your enlightened Self, a vehicle for transportation through the three worlds, matter manifested as a reflection of all that you are and all that you ever will be. The illusion of separation pulling you away from oneness to your very own Self. Drawing your senses, your eyes, your touch, your breath to an unreal world of separative consciousness. This form created by Brahman to experience a world designed for you, for you alone to realise the true nature of your Atman. The Atman, an absolute reflection of Brahman, no less, no more. A perfect Soul. A child of our one true master, whose purpose is to transcend an egoistic idea, a belief that we are parts, that we have difference, that something could be unreal. How can something so beautiful, that invokes such awe and amazement, something as transcendent as a form, which is home to an Enlightened Master, not be Brahman? How can a form such as that not be a truly magnificent reflection of the beauty of my Creator?

Karma Yoga
ENLIGHTENED
I am Enlightened. The burdens of life no longer grip to you, and an awareness of your True Nature is forever present inside. Guiding you, directing your choices, decisions, actions, thoughts and emotions. You are lighter than before, your being transmits an energy of love, reconnecting your Atman to Brahman.

Questions
1.Describe your awareness of Atman.

·Chapter II·

2.How does your Atman enable you to be unaffected by disease, old age or death?
3.Your body is the home of your Enlightened Self. What does this mean?
4.'Matter reflects all that you are.' Can you explain this statement?
5.What is separative consciousness?
6.How is the world designed just for you?
7.Do you experience your soul as perfect?
8.How can you transcend your egoistic ideas?
9.How is your form also Brahman?
10.Describe your own perception of your formed self.

Today: Practice associating your form with Brahman. Ignore the ideas and beliefs of your mind that deny this reality. And stay with the formed reality of your Atman for as long as possible.

Verse 13

Verse
'When the body is light and healthy, when his mind is free from desire, when he has a shining complexion, sweet voice and pleasant odour, when the excretions become scanty, they (realised yogis) say that he has attained the first degree of concentration.'

JnaniYoga
Your body will begin to show signs of your Divinity. An Enlightened Being has no form, the form it takes is only a manifestation of its formless nature. Your perception of an Enlightened Being is directed by your true perception of their Divinity. The two are not separate, but an interconnected whole. Once you begin to realise your True Nature more through meditation practices and studying the scriptures, your own form will commence its transformation. It will begin to reflect your True Nature. This is the power of realisation. Your body will be light and healthy, free from desires. Your complexion will glow, your voice will be sweet and your odour will be pleasant. These are all signs of Enlightenment.

Bhakti Yoga
The beauty pouring out of my being now, its very nature sweet and melodious, radiating a smell so fragrant, so powerful, so alive with new possibilities. The sun shines upon my being, the rays glow through my entire self wakening up the pores of my Soul. My Soul, alive and responsive, bright and alert, speaks to me of blue skies, summer meadows, nature aglow with the wonderment of everything I have become. And, oh Brahman, yes I have become. My becoming is upon me now, so real it is that I feel you so close to me, that I can feel your breath upon my skin.

·Chapter II·

My skin has become a living organism part of the fabric of your nature it shines and glistens, the sparkle of your wisdom and knowledge pouring out for all to see, to know, to experience. A reflection of you, for all to gaze in amazement at your power, your glory. And oh, how glorious you are, you are.

Karma Yoga
BECOMING
The 'ing' beside the word 'become' infers that practice is still required, the journey is ongoing and the destination not yet reached. But, that a sense of becoming, a real, solid belief in your ability to reach the final destination is upon you. And, nothing can stop you now that you have the idea of success.

Questions
1.Have you experienced, or are you experiencing, the signs of first degree concentration mentioned in this verse?
2.Do you listen to Realised Yogis and follow their direction?
3.Can you identify with your inner beauty?
4.Can you feel the sun shining throughout your entire being?
5.Do you experience wonderment towards your Self?
6.Have you become?
7.Can you feel Brahman's breath upon your skin?
8.As you observe your skin, do you see it as a living organism?
9.Can you observe your wisdom and knowledge pouring out of you?
10.Do you recognise how amazing, powerful and glorious you are?

Today: Look in a mirror and study your face, your skin, your eyes. Notice the Divine.

Verse 14

Verse
'Just as a metal disc or a mirror which was stained by dust before, shines brilliantly when it has been cleansed, so also the embodied being (the individual soul, jivatman) realises oneness, attains the end or the goal, and is freed from sorrow when he realises the true nature of the Atman.'

JnaniYoga
The practice of meditation and the study of scriptures, along with the daily rituals performed in worship of Brahman, are leading you towards greater and greater awarenesses of your True Nature. Insights, observations, time spent witnessing who you are becoming, solidify your relationship with your Atman, and it is this

·Chapter II·

strong, unwavering relationship that holds the key to letting go of the past. Letting go of the veil of ignorance that hides your Atman from your awareness. The more you focus on your Atman, the more your false self effortlessly falls away like dust, leaving you cleaner, and more transparent.

Bhakti Yoga
There is so much impurity in the mind - manmade dust that hides the true richness and purity of the Self from the sadhaka. One such as the Divine cannot be tainted by such dust, it only sticks to the reflection of the Self when the Self is identified with the illusion of maya. To realise ones True Nature is to realise that the dust mankind has created and manufactured to hide its True Nature can simply be wiped away with one swipe of the hand directed effortlessly towards the light of Supreme Consciousness. Once consciousness is elevated, raised, transformed to its truest Self it can only but reflect the Atman hidden within.

Karma Yoga
TRANSFORMATION
Transformation is directly related to perception - when something is seen as o ne thing, but then changes into something else entirely, but still retaining the awareness of its initial form, view or perception. The Atman, on being realised, replaces the ego identification that once formed, and was once the basis of all views, opinions and perceptions. Now, the Atman is directing your perception of everything it gazes upon.

Questions
1.How were you stained by the dust of your lower nature?
2.How have you cleansed yourself, and therefore allowed your True Nature to shine forth?
3.Have you realised oneness?
4.Can you describe how your awareness of the Atman frees you from sorrow?
5.What are the mind's impurities?
6.How has your Atman been hidden?
7.'The Divine cannot be tainted by the dust of your lower nature.' How is this possible?
8.Can you stop identifying yourself with the illusion of maya?
9.Is it really that easy to wipe away everything designed to hide your True Nature?
10.Have you experienced your elevated consciousness reflecting the Atman hidden within?

·Chapter II·

Today: As you look in the mirror, see only the Atman reflected back. Realise the dust of your lower nature is but an illusion designed and manufactured. Easy to create and just as easy to destroy.

Verse 15

Verse
'When by means of the real nature of his self the yogi sees, as a lamp, the real nature of Brahman, then having known the unborn, eternal God, who is free from all the modifications of prakriti, he is freed from all fetters or sins.'

JnaniYoga
Once you have met and experienced Brahman, your True Self, the Atman within, and the light of this realisation shines forth just as a lamp inside, a conscience is born, or remembered, within your being. And, this conscience reminds you whenever you are contemplating sin, giving into your lower nature, that you have a choice, another way to go. A separation between your old self, and your Atman has been created. And it is this separation that enables you to choose.

Bhakti Yoga
Nature has a way of burdening herself with manmade modifications, changes to her natural state of being. A beauty so full, rich and pure. A reflection of a Divine hand at play. The colours, the palette of vibrancy and life, the mixtures, the hues of energetic vibration, radiating out through to the canvas of life. The fullness of this beauty a mere illusion for man to fetter away with all kinds of disheartening pranks and maladies. Oh Brahman, what a world we could rejoice in. That world with its technicolour rays of light, so bright and radiant, the greens you have painted, the blues, the earthen colours you have designed for us to realise our True Nature. Our warmth, our own inner vibrancy radiating out of our being. Lost are we that we have fallen away from your ideal, from your creative palette of consciousness. The power you have inside your being to create such wonderment and awe in whomever has the privilege to experience your greatness. We bow down to you, oh Brahman, in reverence and respect for all that you are, and all that you show us to be. We ask that you humbly remove from us the veil of ignorance that hides our True Nature from our minds and hearts. And, that you restore nature back to your intention both within and without.

Karma Yoga
INTENTION
This is not your own intention but God's intention for you. An intention is a choice, a decision made for you within yourself that leads you, guides you, directs you.

·Chapter II·

It has its own energy that pulls you towards the Truth, towards what was meant for you. It is God's will, God's plan, God's ideas and opinions about what is best for you.

Questions
1.Do you see a lamp alight within your being?
2.Does your awareness of Brahman free you from all sin?
3.How have you been modified from your natural state of being?
4.Can you see your energetic vibrations radiating out through you onto the canvas of life?
5.Can you see the world as Brahman intended it to be?
6.Can you describe the creative palette of consciousness?
7.What wonderment and awe have you already created?
8.How can you remove the veil of ignorance that hides your True Nature from your hearts and minds?
9.What is God's intention for you?
10.How are you aligned with God's intention?

Today: Walk in nature and experience the colours, the design, the truth of its Divine intention. Breathe in all you can of its intended Self and have it be a reflection of who you really are.

Verse 16

Verse
'He indeed is the God who pervades all regions. He is the first born (Hiranyagorbha). He has entered into the womb. He alone is born and He will be born. He is inside all persons as the indwelling self, looking everywhere (having his face in all directions).'

JnaniYoga
God intended you to know that your journey here, in the world he created for you, was for you to realise that firstly all this was indeed created for you. There are no mistakes, no accidents, no faults. The creation manifested was, is, and always will be, as it was intended. It is your job to realise this is so, to know that all that was manifested is a part of you, and you are a part of it. There is nothing separating you from another, and therefore all others are you.

Bhakti Yoga
Oh, I can feel you inside me now looking out at all that is us. I see you inside everything and everyone.

·Chapter II·

All people, places and things in the material world are intrinsically connected. A living, breathing, functioning organism, whose blood courses through the veins of all God's creation, Divine love flowing gently and effortlessly, pouring its warmth and calm into all it pervades. The oneness of your creation overwhelms me and leaves me in a breathless state. One of wonderment and awe. Your richness grows and expands through the material world it inhabits, the material world fights back with all its might! But, fight is no longer a reality, no longer a possibility. The love is stronger now, too strong a match for the feeble attempts of resistance. The resistance wanes, until eventually it fades away leaving no trace of its existence. Only the new breath of life can take hold now. Only the new dawn of awakening, to a consciousness so supreme, so sublime, the taste can be felt on the lips of mankind. Humanity finally reaching its resting place, its True Form manifesting for all to see, to feel, to experience, to know that you are inside all. The breath of your life flowing through the blood of your Divine play. Whatever I see, whatever I feel, whatever I experience, whatever I know, is you, and only you. Oh Brahman, bring me back to you, take me to all the places inside of myself where you breathe. Breathe your life over me, let the rivers of love flood through me and let me be you, let me be you. Let it be time, let it be time.

Karma Yoga
CREATION
Creation is the macrocosm of create. When one creates, an intention is developed first, and then this intention is made manifest by design. Therefore, creation is a vast collection of designed manifestations all based on one true intention. This world and its parts are all based on one intention. Each segment, each aspect is connected to and also designed by this intention. You can see an intention when you perceive what it has created. When a man and a woman create a child their intentions can be perceived through the observations of the child . Likewise when God created the world, his intentions could be perceived through observations of the world. If you seek to see, or perceive God's intention for the world , you have to look through his eyes. And, the Atman when experienced enables you to gaze in wonderment at God's creation, and ultimately, his intenti on.

Questions
1.Does God pervade all?
2.How does God enter the womb of all mankind?
3.How is God alone born?
4.How does God see his creation?
5.Can you see that people, places and things are intrinsically connected?
6.Can you explain how the Atman is a living, breathing, functioning organism?

·Chapter II·

7.Can you see the oneness of God's creation?
8.How does the material world fight back at God?
9.Can you imagine a world where humanity finally manifests its True Form?
10.What is God's Divine play?

Today: As you sit quietly and peacefully with your own Self allow your heart to feel the rivers of love, the breath of Brahman, flooding through your veins, until your heart is so full that all you can do is breathe.

Verse 17

Verse
'Salutations, salutations to the God who is in fire, who is in water, who is in the plants, who is in the trees, and who has pervaded the whole universe.'

JnaniYoga
As you experience the world as God intended it to be, and all of creation is perceived as a reflection of you, life becomes easier. A flow occurs, a rhythm. All parts are in harmony as they align themselves with their True Nature . When you think of nature you imagine a consciousness so vast, so connected. A living, breathing organism at one with itself, effortlessly being, with no exertion or manmade constraints. This nature of land, trees, soil, plants etc is a reflection of your own True Nature. The real nature that you were intended to manifest. A tree stands alone in a field. It doesn't enquire into its True Nature, it is itself. It doesn't compare who it is to another, it only sees itself. It doesn't beg for food, it trusts it will be provided for. It is born and dies, without effort. It lives without effort. It is being its intended Self. How are you a reflection of this tree?

Bhakti Yoga
I want to immerse my body in the waters of surrender. I want to lay down my alms, thy weapons of mass destruction. I want to lay down and never be able to rise. I want you to stick me like glue to the floor of your Divine home, and feel my resistance flood out of me onto the carpets of Supreme Consciousness. I need to know you can hear me now, I need to know you are there, that you are always with me. By my side eternally. So that I can rejoice to you, so I can pour the effulgent love out of my heart. I need you to taste my love, smell my love, hear my love, feel my love, see my love. It has grown to be so real inside of my heart that my heart has become transplanted with your grace. Your Grace washes over me, and my Divine Nature permeates the whole universe reaching as far as you allow. Your Grace becomes as real to me now as my past deeds once felt, the depth of your Grace reaches through the trees, the birds, the insects, the sky, the land, the grass

·Chapter II·

are all full now with your touch. The hand that once created all things reaches out through me to experience them. You can see in me now something that once was a flicker, a memory of eternal consciousness awakening in me to all that you designed me to be. An interconnected whole, a part of me in all, and part of all in me. Nothing I touch is not me. Nothing I see is not me. Nothing I smell, taste or hear is not me.

Karma Yoga
EFFORTLESS
The definition of effort is when an action is hard work and requires more energy than you really want to give. Therefore, effortless simply describes a state whereby any action requires no hard work, or labour, and the energy needed to succeed is equal to that one is willing to give. This approach to living life is more natural, but only manifests from your Atman. If you are living from your non-self it will require effort - hard work. If you are living from your Atman not much energy will be expended.

Questions
1.'God is in fire, water, plants and trees.' Explain.
2.What are your alms, weapons of mass destruction?
3.How long can you stay in a state of surrender to God?
4.Can you imagine permanently residing in your Divine home?
5.What does it feel like when your resistance floods out of you?
6.Do you believe God experiences your love for him?
7.Has your heart been transplanted by God's grace?
8.Can you imagine your Divine nature permeating the whole universe?
9.Can you see the Atman in trees, birds, insects, the sky, the land, the grass etc?
10.Imagine you are fluid, flowing through all of God's creation. What does it feel like?

Today: Feel your formed self as fluid, able to flow effortlessly through and in all of God's creations. The land, the animals, the water; the air. The very breath of you is the breath of all.

·Chapter II·

Main Point of Chapter II

THE RELATIONSHIP BETWEEN YOUR MIND AND THE SELF

The main point being conveyed to you throughout Chapter II is about your relationship with your mind from the viewpoint of your SELF. The Self inside all beings must cultivate a deeper, more meaningful understanding of the mind, and its relationship with the Self for Self Realisation to continue. This understanding and knowledge is the second stage of Self Realisation. This understanding starts with consciousness, and an awareness of what it actually is.

The process now has its goal, and the steps to realise this goal are as follows:

a)Making a connection between you and all else.
b)Practice meditation.
c)Develop your awareness.
d)Learn reverence.
e)Worship your Self.
f)Generate states of blissfulness.
g)Transcend mistaken beliefs.
h)Experience beingness.
i)Practice contentment.
j)Experience stillness.
k)Enlightenment.
l)Become who you really are.
m)Transform yourself.
n)Experience your intended Self.
o)Creation.
p)Effortless action.

This chapter outlines, and clearly guides you towards an ever greater experience of how to understand your mind, how to access your innate knowledge and wisdom. And therefore alter your perception to an elevated state of consciousness, seeing all things as Brahman intended.

·Chapter III·

Verse 1

Verse
'He who rules alone by his powers, who rules all the worlds by his powers, who is one and the same at the time of creation and dissolution of the world - they who know him, become immortal.'

JnaniYoga
This verse is reminding you that you will forget God, you will forget your true origin, and ultimately your purpose for existing. And, in this place of forgetfulness you will despair, and it will feel as though you are lost forever in the darkness of your mind that separates you from anything real. But, hope returns when you realise that God is even greater still and has designed this world for you to be and see. And, in this cosmic design he is the director. Everything you need he will provide for you. He knows what you need, where and when. There are no corners, no moments inside this universe that he created that he cannot see. He is omnipresent, omniscient etc. So, whenever you are lost and full of despair he can find you there, and save you from suffering.

Bhakti Yoga
Ego consciousness separates us from our Divine Nature, it breaks away, constantly in a permanent state of dismantling, compartmentalising. It pulls, it snaps, it pushes, it cracks. Until finally we become like little pieces of a never-ending jigsaw puzzle.

·Chapter III·

Until all that we feel that we are, all that we can identify ourselves to be is a tiny piece in a huge jigsaw puzzle. Our identity becomes that one small piece, alone and pained, suffering aimlessly without hope, or freedom. Broken, we submit to a cycle of unending shame and pity that becomes so much of our reality that nothing can convince us otherwise. Despairing and sad we lose all sense of who we are, and our Divine Nature ploughs into the darkness of ignorance and apathy. We are but a fragment of our Selves, alone and frightened we become lost. But, then your grace, your light, touches us ever so gently. We feel the breeze, the air of your warm heart on us and suddenly we awaken, as if from a deep, deep slumber to a knowingness so alive, so heartfelt that we can only but look up, and peering over the burden of self pity we see, no we feel, your compassion. The compassion we once felt before when we were born, when you created our minds, our bodies, our souls as one with yours. And so we cry, we wail, we shout out with relief, with joy, that you came again, and again you came to us. You rescued us from the illusion of separation; from the lies and the deceit. You conquered our hearts with faith and devotion, creating a whole with many parts and the parts have to and must eventually return to their Creator, to be fixed, to be mended, to be soldered together. And then you blew, ever so slightly, on the scars of pain and suffering. And they were gone in a second, no more. Forever yours, forever free, forever alive in you and me. And as the memories of a living death fade away, I see you watching, smiling, reassuringly reminding me of me.

Karma Yoga
COMPASSION

Freedom from despair due to the care and concern of another, who has the power and the glory to set you free, this is the foundation of compassion. It is the will of another to move heaven and earth to ensure your safety. Compassion is an aspect of love, pure Divine love. It is a relative of empathy - one's ability to feel another's pain and suffering as if it were one's own. God feels your pain as if it were his own and can see your pain even when you hide it from yourself. God will free you from any suffering because he cares about you, and doesn't want to see you in pain. But, he can only be compassionate if you let him in to your heart though faith and devotion. He will not go against your will. And, if he knows you are in pain (as he always does), but also sees that you are not realising this pain yourself, he will not interfere in your process of realisation. This is his absolute gift of compassion, offering freedom only when freedom is sought.

Questions

1.How do you experience ego consciousness dismantling, compartmentalising?
2.Are you aware that you are like pieces of a never ending jigsaw puzzle when you do not realise your True Nature?

·Chapter III·

3.Do you identify with feeling like a small piece of a whole?
4.What does it feel like to have no hope?
5.Do you submit to a cycle of shame and pity?
6.Describe being lost.
7.What is it like to suddenly wake up and remember?
8.Do you experience God's compassion?
9.Do you ever cry, wail, shout out with relief that God will rescue you from separation?
10.What does it feel like to know that God is watching you always, to reassure you, to remind you of who you really are?

Today: Know you are part of God's plan, even when you despair, know there is always hope.

Verse 2

Verse

'There is one Audra only who rules all the world by his powers. There is no one beside him who can make him the second. He is present inside the hearts of all beings. He creates all the worlds and maintains and finally withdraws them into himself.'

JnaniYoga

You are in all things, and all things are in you. A quiet voice within the whole of the universe is beckoning you into itself. A journey now you must take towards this voice of oneness. It is the sound of yourself in all things, constantly reminding you of who you are. It is this sound of Supreme Consciousness that resides in all things that you must find and realise. Everything you experience has within it this voice of remembrance and it is your duty to know this truth. Not only is this sound in your realisations of truth, love and oneness, but also in the attachments, desires and relationships you find yourself building. There also you will find that same voice. There is no state of being where this voice of reason, of remembrance does not reside.

Bhakti Yoga

I am not alone anymore, oh Brahman, I am with myself. Myself is more important to me than all the worlds. I dissolve into all matter, all matter dissolves into myself. I cannot leave myself, as myself is all, and all myself. I cannot reside within the hearts of man, and yet my heart is all mankind. Humanity has left an everlasting mark on the being of my entire cosmos. The cosmos is within and without me. Now I am within myself and without myself, I am one without a second.

·Chapter III·

There is nothing that can exist that does not exist without myself. Myself has seen the glory of itself, and has not the power to reject all that I am. I am all that to myself, I am all that to myself, I am all that to myself. Myself, myself, myself. Oh Brahman, I am with you in all ways, at all times, everything you have created is mine, everything you have intended is mine, everything I have become is mine. Oh and I have become, oh Brahman, I have seen, witnessed the becoming of myself into itself and I am. There are no other planes of existence, no other worlds left to conquer, oh and I have conquered, oh Brahman, I have conquered all that you asked of me and more. All that you have set for me, the taste of oneness, Self Realisation, karma, life tests - relationships, attachments and desires. All of these things and more, oh Brahman, I am. I am the oneness, I am the Self Realisation, I am the karma, I am relationships, I am attachments, I am desires. I am, oh Brahman, oh yes I truly am!

Karma Yoga
HUMANITY
Humanity is a manifestation of oneness. Everything is connected by God. The realisation that God is in everything brings human beings to place of connectivity. And, it is in this connectivity that we can find ourselves. Connectivity is the opposite of activity. Activity is generated within when we forget that we are connected. We experience activity inside our minds when we are believing that we are separate from each other. Only when we remember that we are connected by God do we truly experience our humanity. Humanity is: 'Human + Divinity= Humanity.' It is our birth right to know that we were created in God's image with a place for God inside our hearts. And, when we can see ourselves in others, and only then, we can truly see God.

Questions
1.Do you ever feel alone?
2.Can you imagine knowing that you are always with yourself when in the company of others?
3.Do you see yourself in others?
4.Do you reject others because you do not see yourself in them?
5.Can you witness yourself in all when you stand back and observe?
6.What does it mean that there are no planes of existence left to conquer?
7.What life tests does God set for you?
8.What is karma?
9.How are you in attachments, desires and relationships?
10.What is Self Realisation?

·Chapter III·

Today: Know that in all things you are, and you are in all things, from what you deem to be of God, and what you do not, know that you are.

Verse 3

Verse
'That one God having his eyes, his face, arms and feet in every place, when producing heaven and earth, forges them together with his arms and his wings.'

JnaniYoga
The mind separates and distinguishes, it says that something is different, that it is not the same. And, from this one dimensional perception we get caught up in the illusion that we are somehow not connected at all. That we are living in a world that is fearful, where suffering is meaningless and unnecessary. We question God's existence and doubt the reason for our very existence. We are tormented with questions; why are we here, what is the cause. And we become lost, alone and afraid to live, to truly live. We forget to take part in creation, in life. We separate ourselves from creation and despair. But then, we remember through our connection to someone, to something. We wake up, and we feel alive and together. We know who we are, and why we are. We remember God, and life becomes meaningful and purposeful once more.

Bhakti Yoga
We are all one mind, connected and apart, entwined and enmeshed, separate and disconnected. We are all opposites, black and white, hot and cold, dark and light, sweet and sour. We are all one mind and yet we are not. We are all apart and yet we are not. We are all connected and yet we are not. How can we function with all these differences and how can we function with all these similarities? We are all one mind, and yet there is a difference, a difference so real, so alive, so free to wander around in our own minds. And with that freedom comes solitude, comes separation, comes lack, arrogance and alienation. We are not the same, on the outside where our mind falls upon an unrealness. We are different sizes, different colours, different genders, different ages. But, if we go beyond the difference that our mind sees, we can find a sameness. A light, a desire, a warmth, a closeness, a connection, a yearning, a faith, a devotion to something so vast and expansive, so complex and intricate that our minds cannot fathom or comprehend. And, when we go beyond to this inner being we are wrapped tightly in the arms and wings of Gods. And their beckoning to come home, to come home to the realisation of one-ness, of sameness, to that major glitch in the matrix of the mind, that states that we are all one and that our differences are no longer what ties us together to

·Chapter III·

anything or anyone. But, it is our sameness, our light, that abundantly steers us together to bridge the gaps our minds always forge and to reconnect to that bigger, much larger, reality called the Divine. And, to bask in the glory of our connection and to be in that oneness again, with love, happiness and kindness to all of God's creatures and to all mankind.

Karma Yoga
SAMENESS
If you look past noticeable differences such as physical appearances, life choices and relationships and you actually feel aware of the Atman in others, you instantly know, or remember, that nothing is different. Because what is true, and real is actually like God. Sameness means like God. Everything is like God, everything can be identified as God.

Questions
1.'We are all one mind.' How does this make you feel?
2.Describe your opposites.
3.How are you different from others?
4.How are you the same as others?
5.When you focus on difference how does it make you feel?
6.Do you know when your mind is seeing the unreal?
7.Can you ever experience going beyond the difference?
8.Do you ever realise oneness in your life?
9.What is the light that bridges the gaps your mind forges?
10.Do you ever feel a kindness to all of God's creatures, and to all mankind?

Today: Look beyond differences and see the God in all of God's creation.

Verse 4

Verse
'May Audra, the creator and supporter of the Gods, the great seer, the Lord of all, who created at first Hiranyagarbha, endow us with good thoughts (pure intellect).'

JnaniYoga
You will observe, witness and perceive truths now. They will appear separate your reality, and yet they will connect you to an even greater reality. One you could only imagine was possible. Time must be spent in this witnessing state, observing all your experiences from a comfortable difference.

·Chapter III·

And, as you witness, you will know that that one Truth belongs with God. And, you will desire to know God more.

Bhakti Yoga
I am not what I am anymore, I am not where I am, I am not when I am, but I am who I am? Who am I, oh Brahman, who am I? Am I that you that I know to be in all things at all times? Am I that you that is free to travel through space and time, to yearn through distance and beckon forth a time once forgotten? A time where all can be seen through the eyes of yours, the eyes of mine. Oh, what a sight to be held, a thought to be conquered. One of power, of glory! I see the eyes of mine with the flicker of a flame at the centre, a flame of knowledge grows from a fire burning inside me that will never go out. A flame of remembering that we travel through time, our eyes so large and alive with the knowingness that time stands still for us, and in that time our moments last forever, forever, forever.

Karma Yoga
KNOWINGNESS
Knowingness is the feeling deep within your heart that God is real, and is existing always for you to know him. It is a longing and yearning for more and more truth. It is a state of Supreme Consciousness that just is. No explanation, no reason, no logic. It just is.

Questions
1.What are thoughts?
2.How can thoughts be Divine?
3.Have you ever experienced pure thoughts?
4.Have you ever felt you know who you are?
5.What does the question, 'Who am I?' mean to you?
6.What is space and time?
7.What is this sense of time that has been forgotten?
8.How does one conquer 'thought'?
9.What is the experience of 'time standing still'?
10.How does consciousness travel, and yet never move?

Today: Consciousness travels through time and space and yet is always still, never moving. Consider this, reflect on this, and remember this.

·Chapter III·

Verse 5

Verse
'O Audra, with thy form which is auspicious, which is not dreadful, and which manifests what is holy, with that all-blessed form, appear to us, 0 dweller among the mountains.'

JnaniYoga
The Mountain of the Highest Truth must be conquered. You will travel up the mountain, and back to base continuously for all eternity, until you realise the mountainous peak that must be conquered. The mountainous peak is your goal of Self Realisation. It is reaching upwards, beyond your limited mind, to a higher point within that same mind. It is your goal to stay at this place of Truth for as long as possible.

Bhakti Yoga
Oh Brahman, the ever living on the highest, the highest, the highest. All mountains I have climbed to reach the greatest heights ever known. To bravely go where all else fails to know, the top I have claimed as thine own. I have reached, and when I have fallen, once more I strive for ever more to know, to be. Remember that this glory is to be had by all. The all of which that I am. Speaking is ignorant of knowing, that all that is ever needed is to reach and then be still. To conquer, to claim the highest truth here, the truth that is always freely given, the truth that calls our name now, but can never truly be spoken. That you and I are dreaming, dreaming of a space in time, a space where we are weeping for the whole of our beloved mankind.

Karma Yoga
TRUTH
Truth is knowing that nothing is real but God. Therefore, truth is knowing that this is factual, and never changes. It is a permanent reality, a permanent state of being when all is only seen as God. Truth can be experienced, and lost. But, truth must be known, and to know truth one must believe everything else to be unreal. Everything appearing to be real is a lie, and one must have courage to stay in the presence of truth above all else.

Questions
1.How does God dwell amongst the mountains?
2.What is mean by highest?
3.What mountains have you climbed?
4.What heights have you reached?

·Chapter III·

5.Do you experience yourself as brave?
6.Do you feel alone, when others are not climbing this mountain with you?
7.What is it like to claim the top of the Mountain of Truth as your own?
8.When you fall from truth, how do you strive to know more?
9.Can you describe the stillness at the top of the mountain?
10.What does it mean to weep for our beloved mankind?

Today: Reach up beyond your limiting mind, and conquer the space that holds the highest truth there, the space where God and you are one.

Verse 6

Verse
'O Lord of the mountains! Make propitious the arrow which thou holdest in thy hand to shoot. Do not hurt man or the world, 0 mountain protector.'

JnaniYoga
God is the Lord, and Protector of the Absolute Truth. He created a world for us to conquer, and realise his True Nature and our own are one. We must realise that God holds the Truth, and protects it from harm. He will not allow any man to stain, or tarnish this Truth under his protection. We must not allow anyone to harm this Truth. We must protect this Truth at all times. There will be times, moments, experiences that challenge our knowledge and beliefs thus far. We must take responsibility for these realisations, and protect them from judgement or condemnation.

Bhakti Yoga
I brave the terrain of forgetfulness for you, oh Brahman, and only you. Only you could bring forth the courage within that I must summons now to face the rocky regions. The rocky regions of unknowing that man clambers upon, falling, failing, stumbling. I can, more ever so, to reach where they must go. To strain, to stretch, to reason, to push when they go slow.

Karma Yoga
COURAGE
Courage is to have the willingness and the skills to bravely fight injustice of any kind. It is the realisation that fighting, challenging anything that appears to be a threat to God, is necessary, and acceptable. Courage is a strong will to do the right thing even if, and especially if, everyone else is against that choice. You must summon up all your will and strength to fight the demons of disbelief both within and without.

·Chapter III·

Questions

1.Who is the Lord of the Mountains?
2.How does this Mountain Protector, protect man and the world?
3.What is the terrain of forgetfulness?
4.What does it mean to be brave?
5.How does God bring forth your courage from within?
6.What are the rocky regions of unknowing?
7.How does man fail, falter and stumble?
8.How do you reach where all man must go?
9.How do you strain, stretch and reason yourself across this rocky terrain?
10.How do you push when they go slow?

Today: Whenever you fall into forgetfulness of who you truly are, hear the sound of the breath of the one that carries you across the rocky terrain.

Verse 7

Verse

'Higher than this personal God is the supreme Brahman, who is infinite, who is concealed within all beings according to their bodies and who is the only pervader of the whole universe. By knowing him as Lord one becomes immortal.'

JnaniYoga

Your consciousness, being the same as Brahman's through the awareness and realisation of your Atman, has no form, and yet it moves effortlessly within all form. To realise this fundamental reality you will have to imagine yourself inside all forms, and feel as though you can perceive yourself quite literally looking out from this form. And, taking into consideration your perception that stems from these observations, you will have to imagine yourself merged with all things, and remove the belief that all things have seams, and are separate.

Bhakti Yoga

I can merge now, my consciousness and yours are one. Never could I have imagined the endlessness of your mighty charge. The power we share between us does pervade the entire universe. I am experiencing this universe inside me, I have lost all sense of my shape. My being has become quite formless and spreads itself right through. I cannot see the ends now, the sides have been removed, the formlessness of my being I feel is on the move. It moves without me knowing, it really is no effort to become the ever knowing of all that can be seen.

·Chapter III·

The unseen is as real, and doesn't change at all; form, anything tangible in my vision that I once could not fathom for fear that if I knew it, it would not be the same. And then the ever knowing would not be real for me.

Karma Yoga FORMLESS
Your being is light, energy, consciousness, bliss. The physical matter that has manifested in this physical reality is only a projection of your unmanifested self. What is actually perceived is in fact your true state, that is without a physical representation, and this state is without form. This is your True Nature .

Questions
1.Who is your personal God?
2.How does your personal God enable you to realise your True Nature?
3.'The Supreme Brahman is infinite.' What does this mean?
4.How do you merge?
5.How is your consciousness one with Brahman?
6.What is the power you share with Brahman?
7.What does it feel like to lose all sense of your shape?
8.How does your formlessness move without you knowing?
9.How do you experience the unseen as real?
10.'Everything tangible in your vision is the same as Brahman.' Explain what this means.

Today: See how much formlessness you can realise in your own being.

Verse 8

Verse
'I know this mighty being (Purusha) who shines effulgent like the sun beyond darkness. One passes beyond death only by knowing him. There is no other road for obtaining liberation.'

JnaniYoga
Only with a relationship with a personal God can you now continue. This relationship must be strong and real. It must be the foundation of all that you do, feel and think. If you do not develop, cultivate and strengthen this relationship you will experience feeling lost much more often, and the process of Self Realisation will be slowed down considerably.

·Chapter III·

Bhakti Yoga

Around and around I go, looking everywhere and going nowhere. Obtain nothing have I, oh Brahman the ever being. One door closes and another door opens. I find myself lost looking for something, and yet nothing do I find. I cannot find anything, for you have locked me out. The keys I cannot find. The keys to unlock the one true door, the door to freedom. I am bound now in a darkness, a cold dungeon of fear and lovelessness. I have everything that I could ever find beyond the doors that opened. And yet, I have nothing I want, I need, I crave, I desire, I lust, I beg, I find I have nothing. I am empty. I am empty. I am empty. Fill me up, let me in. Open the door, show me the key. The key, the key, the key. Oh Brahman, my dearest Brahman, let me in, open the door, show me the way. The path I must find, I must follow my own path, I must walk alone along the road that leads to a place I do not know. A place I am destined to find, and still a place that alludes me. I cannot reach where you want me to go, I cannot strive ever more for you, I cannot stride out to distant lands, without you. How do I reach a place I do not know, and have never been to, without you? Show me the way, take me by the hand and lead me there. I will go wherever you need, wherever you say, wherever I must. I will go there today with you, only with you.

Karma Yoga
LIBERATION

Only God can set you free from the bondage of your unrealised nature. Freedom from bondage can only be granted to you by God. The nature, and meaning, of liberation is to literally set free. This infers that someone or something is freeing you. It is not yourself, but Brahman alone, that has the power to liberate you from this separative existence.

Questions

1.What shines effulgent like the sun, and is beyond darkness?
2.What is beyond death?
3.'Only by knowing God can you obtain liberation.' Do you know this statement to be true?
4.Can you feel the despair of being lost and alone?
5.Can you recognise that there are so many unopened doors for you to unlock to gain liberation?
6.Do you have the humility that only Brahman has the keys?
7.Do you walk your path alone, or holding God's hand?
8.How can you reach a place that you do not know?
9.Do you feel desperately in need of God to show you the way?
10.How does it feel to be by God's side?

·Chapter III·

Today: Know with all certainty that you cannot realise yourself alone, you must be by the side of God to know exactly where you must go.

Verse 9

Verse
'There is nothing higher than or different from him, nothing greater or more minute than him. He alone stands in the heaven like a tree, one without a second and immoveable. The whole world is filled by that being.'

JnaniYoga
Now is the time to cultivate and practice building a deeper, more trusting relationship with your inner eye, as opposed to your external two eyes. The two eyes that you use daily can be misleading; they can see a snake where a rope lies. Only the inner eye once realised can give an accurate account of what you are looking at. Only your inner eye can truly know what is real. Once realised nothing will ever deceive you again.

Bhakti Yoga
I must look beyond now, and beyond all darkness there lives a light. A light so bright my eyes can no longer see. My vision impaired by light, closes its material eyes and opens an eye I did not know was there. An eye that I can now see through, an eye that shows me things I did not know existed. These things of reality beyond my material eyes show me a world I could only have imagined before. I see the world now as it was intended by you, for us. I see that there were, and are, no mistakes. I see a perfect world, one of light, an energy, it radiates and spreads right through. It connects all things to each other. It draws all darkness inside and the light wipes it clean. This is a world. This is your world. This is our world.

Karma Yoga
REALITY
'Real+ Divinity= Reality.' Real is everything experienced that is solid and factual, and Divinity is everything experienced that is manifested from God. Therefore, reality is everything experienced that is a solid fact manifested by God. The opposite of reality is 'Real + Activity = Reactivity'. Therefore, anything manifested by man's belief in separation.

Questions
1.Do you believe there is nothing higher or different from God?
2.How do you look beyond darkness?

·Chapter III·

3.Does the light of Supreme Consciousness make you close your eyes and go inside?
4.Have you experienced your inner eye opening?
5.How do you perceive things differently from your physical eyes?
6.Do you feel in awe of the world seen by your inner eye?
7.How did God intend for you to see the world?
8.Can you see that there are no mistakes in the world?
9.How does your inner eye draw all the darkness inside?
10.How does the light wipe clean all darkness?

Today: Sit awhile and close your eyes. As you sit, trust an inner eye will open and allow you to see the world as it really is. The world that was intended for you.

Verse 10

Verse
'That which is beyond this world is without form and without suffering. Those who know it become immortal, but others instead suffer pain only.'

JnaniYoga
It is not possible to be in remembrance of God at all times, as this is only possible when Full Realisation has occurred. So, you must have a plan, that needs to be created whilst in a state of remembrance for the times you will fall into the darkness. First, you must accept that darkness will come even though this will be a painful reality, you must be courageous enough to be honest with yourself. Then, you must create reminders for yourself in your life, that when seen will be hard to deny, even when you are full of sensory activity. And finally, above all these tools and attributes that you manifest, you will have to be patient with yourself.

Bhakti Yoga
Who are you Brahman? What are you Brahman? That you can create such a world, and yet the creator is nowhere to be seen. Do you have form that can be reached by mere man, mere mortals? I think not, I know not of your becoming. The material eye that you created to see all that is not you, to create an experience of something in order for that experience to know nothing. How can nothing be known? To know what you are I must know what you are not. I know now that you are nothing. There, and only there, you can be found. In all the searching and in all the lost places we collect so many moments of fullness. Our minds and our hearts burst forth with this fullness. Our beings, they are so full we could explode like a bomb of sensory activity.

·Chapter III·

And then, with your Grace, that we have earned by facing our darkest fear that really you do not exist, by your Grace we are released from the bondage of fullne ss, and in the nothingness you are there, we find you. You had been there always, patiently knowing we would come, trusting us that we would find our way back with your Grace, only with your Grace, with your Grace.

Karma Yoga
PATIENCE
'Pay+ Conscience= Patience.' There will be times when you despair, and become critical of your own capacity for Realisation. This is one of the worst of human defects. The ability to give oneself a really hard time, to say mean things to oneself, to be self-hating, self-depreciating. These are signs that God has been forgotten. If you listen to your conscience, and pay attention to what it says you will know that this is unacceptable behaviour towards yourself. So, consistently pay attention to your conscience and be still, remain in the moment and breathe. This is when all will be well.

Questions
1.Who, and what, is Brahman?
2.Do you ever acknowledge feeling angry towards God?
3.What do you do when you feel abandoned by God?
4.Do you question the process of Self Realisation, and doubt its validity?
5.Do you ever push yourself to see God in bad experiences?
6.What is it like to be in a state of fullness due to sensory activity?
7.Do you avoid sensory activity?
8.Do you ever feel God does not really exist? Why does this happen?
9.When you return to a state of nothingness do you easily remember God again?
10.How does it feel to know that God trusts you, and believes you can find your way back to him?

Today: Be aware of just how full your being has become of unnecessary sensory activity. Your mind full of thoughts, your heart full of emotions. And sit awhile with this painful reality.

Verse 11

Verse
'He (the Lord) is the face, the head and neck of all. He dwells in the heart of all beings. He pervades all. Therefore he is omnipresent and propitious.'

·Chapter III·

JnaniYoga
Through patience and hard work you will start to hear a quiet voice in times of forgetfulness. It will be like an anchor for you, rooting you to the consciousness of God. This voice of conscience will pull you back into the arms of nothingness once more. The sound of your conscience will vibrate within all of your sensory activity, so it can no longer completely grip onto you. This will make the times of forgetting much shorter than before.

Bhakti Yoga
Oh my Brahman, oh how I have missed you. Oh how I yearn for more of you. To know now that you are there inside me always, I so dearly desire to be back with you. And yet again I find myself in this place of fullness, but this place that once felt so lifeless, so dull, so meaningless and so helpless - now I feel a difference. You have charmed my heart and mind. A spell has been placed upon my being. Once felt I can no longer indulge in forgetfulness. I realise that you are inside me now, and in all things that I create you are there. You have touched my heart and whenever I think, you are in my thoughts, whenever I feel, you are in my emotions, whenever I am, you are in my being forever, forever, forever.

Karma Yoga
NOTHINGNESS
Nothingness is a state of mind. It is experienced within your own mind, and can be likened to light. Light is the closest to describing nothingness. Words cannot describe nothingness, and/or its meaning. And, attempts should not be made to do so. Except to explain that when you do experience it, you will automatically know what it is. And, realise it cannot be explained. This is its nature, without explanation.

Questions
1.What dwells inside your own heart?
2.What pervades all?
3.Explain 'omnipresent' and 'propitious'.
4.What is it like to miss God?
5.How do you yearn more for God?
6.Do you desire to be back with God?
7.Do you experience the fullness of sensory activity differently now?
8.Has God charmed your heart and mind?
9.How is Brahman in all things that you create?
10.Do you hear the quiet whisper of Brahman calling you back home?

·Chapter III·

Today: Know that once you have experienced the nothingness of Brahman, you can never go back to the despair of a full heart and mind. You will always hear the quiet whisper of Brahman calling you back home.

Verse 12

Verse
'That person (Purusha) is indeed the great Lord. He controls everything. He is light. He is everlasting. He guides the intellect of all beings in order to enable them to attain that extremely pure state (moksha).'

JnaniYoga
So, now you will have realised that you need to learn more about what Brahman really is. You will have to study, to research, and search for knowledge from what has been known by others, and what is known by you. This is absolutely necessary, and you will be keen to learn, because without Brahman guiding you, you will fail.

Bhakti Yoga
I no longer am in need of those transient sensory moments that I once craved. I search now, ever greater still for knowledge , the knowledge of you, oh Brahman. You have cast your mighty spell of yearning, it resides now within my mind and I crave the knowledge of you. I journey inside my own mind, I search for the light of you, the light of you that shines so bright to guide me back to thee. I will leave no stone unturned. I will tread ever so carefully upon the rocky road of intellect and I will come home, I will reach you. My mind, I know now it desires your light, your guidance, your beauty. It works for you and only you. The light of you has become my beacon, and my mind it draws towards. Oh Brahman, I am coming, I am coming, I am coming.

Karma Yoga
LIGHT
Light is the energy generated by realisations. The more realisations, the more light. This light radiates throughout your mind, and illuminates the path that you must follow. So, to realise your True Nature and continue on your path of Self discovery you need more light. Each realisation generates a certain amount of light, equal to the value of the realisation. The energy of realisations (light) can only be generated by digging deep holes in the storehouse of knowledge within .

Questions
1.'God is in control.' How does this make you feel?

·Chapter III·

2.'God guides your intellect.' Explain what this means?
3.What is 'moksha'?
4.What is it like to no longer be so attached to transient, sensory moments?
5.How do you search for knowledge?
6.How does your mind yearn, and how does it differ from the heart yearning?
7.Do you crave knowledge?
8.How is the intellect a rocky road?
9.Can you imagine your mind only working for God?
10.Can you see your mind as it draws towards the beacon of light within it?

Today: See the light of knowledge in your own mind as it beckons you forth to yearn for more.

Verse 13

Verse
'The Purusha of the size of a thumb, who is concealed by the heart, intellect and mind, always dwells in the heart of creatures as their inner self. Those who know him become immortal.'

JnaniYoga
The light of knowledge will always return you to the heart. You must be willing to return to the heart, and not get attached to acquiring knowledge. Too much knowledge without heart can be just as painful as no knowledge.

Bhakti Yoga
The knowledge I have found, it has brought me to a place and here I find myself. It is in my heart now that I am, that you are ever with me. I experience you, a pulsating rhythm so powerful and immeasurable that is imploding onto the page of life. The life has become a heartbeat, and the heart of my life, it beats so fast. The vastness of this power, it yearns for you even more, a restlessness has taken over me, a need has risen inside of me, a need for you. I am needing you now, I am needing you now.

Karma Yoga
NEED
A desperate pain, so vast, so excruciating, it drives you, controls you, maddens you deeply. It pushes you with great force towards Enlightenment. It is a relentless force for God. A deep longing for more and more realisations. This energy is made manifest only by the heart that lies within the Inner Self. The hearts longing when felt compels you to move all obstacles. It is your driving force.

·Chapter III·

Questions
1.Do you believe your Inner Self dwells in your heart?
2.'Knowing your Inner Self frees you from the cycle of birth and death.' Discuss this.
3.Where does knowledge take you?
4.Where do you find your Self?
5.Describe being in your heart?
6.Describe the pulsating rhythm that is so powerful and immeasurable.
7.How does your heart affect your life?
8.How vast is the power generated from your heart?
9.Describe the restlessness?
10.Experience the need for God.

Today: Acknowledge the greatest need you have is for God.

Verse 14

Verse
'The person (Purusha) has a thousand heads, a thousand eyes and a thousand feet. He envelops the whole world on all sides and extends beyond it by ten fingers breadth.'

JnaniYoga
Excitement is upon you now. An excitement that leaves you breathless. You need to experience this excitement, validate it, and acknowledge where it comes from, and where it is taking you.

Bhakti Yoga
This beating heart of everlasting consciousness, it is in my eyes, my ears, my nose, my mouth, my hands and my feet. It has exploded now into my life. I can no longer control my yearning for your touch, your smile, your smell, your gaze. My heart is beating so fast, my pores are sweating with yearning. My mind, it is pulling so hard towards you. I can no longer control myself. I can no longer feel my old self, my old restraints have dissolved and I am compelled without reasoning forwards, upwards, onwards. I will reach you, I must, I cannot falter. One step without you is misery to me. The idea of not being with you I can no longer bear. I must have you, with all my might I must push myself upon you, regardless. I must push myself towards to you without constraint. I must push myself, myself, myself.

·Chapter III·

Karma Yoga
YEARNING
Obsession with God. Completely addicted to God. Lusting after God. Every moment is filled with this desire for God. This is yearning.

Questions
1.Does God envelop the whole world?
2.Can you feel everlasting consciousness?
3.Do you feel consumed by God?
4.Has God exploded into your life?
5.Do you try to control your yearning for God?
6.Does your heart beat fast for God?
7.Do you feel your mind pulling you towards your heart?
8.Describe the misery of being without God.
9.Do you push yourself upon God?
10.Do you let go, and be fearless, in your quest for God?

Today: Allow yourself to completely let go and fearlessly push yourself towards God.

Verse 15

Verse
'That person alone (Purusha) is all this, what has been and what will be. He is also the Lord of immortality. He is whatever grows by food.'

JnaniYoga
You will start to begin to feel as though Realisation is possible. And, that believing it was impossible is laughable now. Doubts and fears will still grow inside. But, this solidarity of knowing will quickly take over and you will return to your heart with speed.

Bhakti Yoga
Oh my God, I have become. I am all that I am, I am you. I have pushed myself and now I find myself inside you. No longer on the outside yearning. I am inside now, and the power that wells up inside my being, the enormity of it. And yet, it is an experience so normal to me, that I am not outside of it. One without a second have I become. And knowing that I am is so real. There is a peacefulness here that one cannot describe, and one must try. I must make all attempts to share this place with you, to be on the inside now, beckoning you forth towards me. A surrealness, a moment of realness, an experience of absolute certainty that

how could I have ever thought, believed, that this wasn't real. It feels so obvious now, to sit inside you. Once realised the obviousness of this reality makes me want to laugh with the lightness of this reality that so eluded me, for so long. I am, I am, I am.

Karma Yoga
CERTAINTY
Certainty is the capacity to say, and know, 'I am that.' Of course, Full Realisation has not been actualised, but I know I'm going home, and nothing can deter me, nothing can stand in my way. I have had enough times of experiencing myself now, I am nearly half way there. I have turned a corner, and can see the road before me as clearly as the light of day.

Questions
1.How does it feel to know that you are all that is, all that has been, and all that ever will be?
2.What grows by food?
3.Can you say, 'I am'?
4.'You're on the inside now.' How does it feel?
5.Do you feel enormous power within?
6.Does your power feel normal now?
7.Are you peaceful?
8Do you share this place with others?
9.Do you think it laughable that you once thought Realisation eluded you?
10.Do you know Self Realisation resides in us at all times?

Today: Know that Self Realisation comes to us all, and yet it resides in us all at all times.

Verse 16

Verse
'With hands and feet everywhere, with eyes, heads and mouth everywhere, with ears everywhere, that exists encompassing everything in the world.'

JnaniYoga
You are nearly half way towards realising your True Nature, when the previous lessons have been realised you can rest awhile and reflect on the true nature of Self Realisation. What it actually is? What it really means? This is a time of deep inner reflection, where you can ponder on all that has been, and realise what is needed to become. It is a moment created by God, for God, so that you can

·Chapter III·

bring all your insights and awarenesses together as one.

Bhakti Yoga
The hands, feet, eyes, heads, mouths, and ears of all mankind belong to the Lord of Supreme Consciousness. No one is separate from this Divine plan. Those amongst us with limited vision seek to Self Realise when they return home; where is home? Is home not here and now? Why wait for something that may never happen? Why not create the experience of oneness now in this very moment? Merge back with the Divine now, experience Samadhi now. Close your eyes, ears and mouth. Imagine everyone, all of mankind, with you doing the same thing. Now imagine the space inside of you and the space inside them is the same. Imagine that the inner space of all is connected, there is nothing that separates it. Now imagine the interconnected inner space of all is connected to the source of all creation, the consciousness of supreme power and might. Now feel that connection grow inside as you focus and feel that inner connection with all that is and all that will ever be. This is the starting point to Self Realisation.

Karma Yoga
SAMADHI
The Realisation that everything is within your own being. All of creation, the whole universe is in you. The consciousness of your Self travels throughout all of existence, and yet never moves. It is an inner state of Absolute Realisation, and in this state there is nothing outside of it. Only you exist. There is no second.

Questions
1.Do you realise that all hands, feet, eyes, heads, mouths and ears are your own?
2.'You are mankind.' What does this mean?
3.What is the Divine plan?
4.How can you Self Realise when you return home, when home is where you must realise?
5.Where is home?
6.Have you experienced Samadhi?
7.Can you imagine the whole of mankind doing the same thing at the same time?
8.Can you believe your inner space is the same as all others?
9.Do you feel connected to all that is?
10.Do you believe you have started to Self Realise?

Today: Spend your day cultivating not only an awareness of this inner connection, but a feeling of oneness in your being. When your mind becomes active stop what you are doing and look around in your environment and feel yourself connected to everything in that environment.

·Chapter III·

Feel your consciousness merge with everything that is and everything that ever will be.

Verse 17

Verse

'He shines forth with the qualities of all the senses, yet he is devoid of all the senses. He is the Lord of all, the ruler of all, the refuge of all and the friend of all.'

JnaniYoga

It is time to tackle your five senses. This is a scary time when doubts and fears will rear up again into your mind. But, it is necessary for future realisations that you face your sensory activity fearlessly. The idea is that you can use your five senses for God, or for your ego. And, now is the time to explore the difference. The easiest sense to begin with is your eyes. Your eyes take in so much information every second. Learn the difference between how your eyes see God, and how they see the ego. Notice through your observations how different the experience is, and how the differing experiences affect your mind, your heart and your life.

Bhakti Yoga

Everything we see around us is a reflection of the One True Creator. Everything we see, hear, feel and touch is at one with that creative energy. Nothing is separate. The creative energy lives and breathes inside all things, perfectly in harmony with itself, perfectly at peace, perfectly at one. The Divine hand at play in all creation is reflected back to us through our five senses. Our mind plays tricks with us and does not see the beauty, the oneness, the freedom that creative energy gives freely to us in every moment, in everything.

Karma Yoga

CREATIVE

Creative is one's ability to manipulate, to mould something into whatever shape you desire. This ability can be used with matter, consciousness and also energy. You can literally mould consciousness into any form you want. This capacity to manipulate is not derived from the negative use of the term. But, the positive aspect. Just as with clay, you can mould it at will into any shape you imagine or intend it to be. So too with consciousness, you can manipulate it to create whatever you will.

·Chapter III·

Questions

1.How does God have the qualities of all the senses?
2.How is God devoid of all the senses?
3.Do you know God is the Lord, refuge, ruler and friend of all?
4.How is everything you see a reflection of the One True Creator?
5.How are our five senses related to creative energy?
6.Does the creative energy live and breathe inside all things?
7.How is creative energy in harmony, at peace, at one with itself perfectly?
8.How does the Divine hand play out in all creation?
9.Does your mind play tricks, if so how?
10.Can you move your consciousness inside things at will?

Today: Breathe consciously. Relax and let go of all misconceptions and illusions. Drive yourself closer to the source. Move your consciousness inside everything around you, feel at one with it, listen to it, speak to it, hear it. It is your friend, your ruler. Go past the form of all and breathe effortlessly into the reality inside every living thing. Listen to its heartbeat, that heartbeat is yours, it is you. Feel it, connect with it, be at one with yourself.

Verse 18

Verse

'He dwells in the body, the city of nine gates. He is the soul (Hamsa) who sports in the outside world. He is the controller of the whole world, both the stationary and the moving.'

JnaniYoga

It is true that once you reach this level place of knowing yourself that you are protected. All the knowledge you have accumulated thus far is safe, and can never be lost again. If you have practiced and worked very hard, and can truly say that you have mastered all the previous verses, then I can assure you that your realised state up to now is completely protected. And, that you should take a moment to digest and accept this reality, this guarantee from God.

Bhakti Yoga

My soul is yours, my soul and your soul are one. We can play, we can laugh, we can dance, we can sing and all the while we are doing nothing at all. The unrealness of this world has become one with our reality and anything we experience can no longer touch us. Whatever we do from this point forth will no longer seep into our pores. To think that something is real is the only way it can manifest as matter in our entire being.

·Chapter III·

Just as a swan plays in the water we, our souls, are free to play in the water of life and the realisation of the unreality of this formed existence becomes like the feathers of a swan, a sheath of knowledge so thick and real that the water of life can no longer get passed our remembering. Just as the water the swan plays in is unable to absorb past the protective coating, the realisation has now become my protection from the small minded, limited belief that anything of this world can move such an immovable object as the Self.

Karma Yoga
PROTECTION
A guarantee that all your hard work, all the effort you have expelled realising your True Nature is now safe and that God is your guardian. He will ensure that nothing will be lost or forgotten.

Questions
1.Do you feel safe now?
2.Can you relax more, and enjoy your journey?
3.Is God protecting you? How do you know?
4.Do you feel untouchable, invincible?
5.What does it mean that only if it is believed to be real can it exist?
6.Does life seem like a game now that you can play?
7.Are you aware of your protective sheath of knowledge?
8.Can you feel that life's situations are finding it hard to reach inside and affect you?
9.Have you let go of small minded, limited beliefs in relation to what is real?
10.Do you realise that Realisation of the Self is a protection of itself?

Today: Know that you are protected from this unreality of this world only by Realisation of the Self.

Verse 19

Verse
'Without hands and feet he goes fast and grasps; without eyes he sees; without ears he hears. He knows all that is to be known, yet there is none who knows him. They call him the first, the great person.'

JnaniYoga
At this point, and with the accumulated energy of all that you have learnt, you can express the senses of consciousness that will be manifesting effortlessly from your being. These senses of consciousness are love, empathy, compassion,

·Chapter III·

selflessness etc. Practice sharing these qualities with whomever you meet. And, as you do so, you will see more of God reflected back to you, which will further propel you forwards on your path.

Bhakti Yoga
Without love we are nothing, absolutely nothing. We are loveless beings in a loveless world. Without love we are devoid of senses, free to do as we choose and yet bandaged by the selfishness of egoism. We are free to be carefree and free to loose all our grip on a senseless reality. We need love to be, to know, to feel, to think. Without love we cannot live or survive this senseless existence at all. We need love to be who we are. It feeds our senses of egoless existence. We are free to choose that which has always been and will always be. That which is our birthright, our karma. To know ourselves and our intrinsic nature. It is at one with the Divine. We are the first, the last, the everything. Nothing exists without us. We are one and all. Nothing can survive without our very breath, our heartbeat of Divine consciousness wills us on, to know, to be, to breathe, to live, to feel.

Karma Yoga
THE SENSES
Love, selflessness, empathy, compassion etc, are the senses of Divinity. They work within the same basic principles of the ego's five senses, but there are many more of them, too many to mention. They reside, attached to your True Self (your Atman), and take in even more information per second than your physical senses. They are how you relate to the real world, and are used to perceive what is in your environment. For example: When you are selfless towards another, your perception is altered, and the information you receive is affected by this new perception.

Questions
1.Are you a great person?
2.'Without love you are nothing.' Explain.
3.Do you experience lovelessness?
4.'Without love you are devoid of Divine senses.' Explain.
5.Are you bandaged by the selfishness of your ego?
6.Are you carefree?
7.Do you need love to survive?
8.Do you need love to be who you really are?
9.What is your karmic birthright?
10.How does the heartbeat of Divine consciousness will you on?

Today: Sit and breathe in all that you are, all that you will ever be. Sit and

·Chapter III·

take in yourself. Your ve,y nature is consciousness, pure and Divine, loving, caring, selfless, giving, freedom, ecstasy. Breathe all you can breathe in of yourself. Know that you are at one with the Divine hand that made you to be. Let go of, free yourself of, the bondage of Divine karma. You willed it into existence, you can will it inside yourself once more, to merge effortlessly with your Self. Senses are not only in ego, senses are a/so in consciousness. These senses of Divinity are love, empathy, compassion, selflessness etc. Devote more time to these, less to the senses of five external organs, and more to the organ of your soul!

Verse 20

Verse
'Subtler than even the subtlest and greater than the greatest, the Atman is hidden in the heart of the creature. One becomes free from all grief and desires, by the grace of the desireless creator, and realises him as the Great Lord.'

JnaniYoga
Do you only allow yourself to express your Divine senses of love, selflessness, compassion, empathy etc, to a chosen few? Do you only share with man, or do you express your Divinity to all creatures, all of creation? Now it is long overdue, that you share your Divinity with all of God's creation. And stop limiting yourself to a few. Expand your Divinity, reach those less fortunate than yourselves: animals, nature, the poor, the suffering. Practice sharing yourself with all you meet, all you encounter.

Bhakti Yoga
Bhakti law states that one realises the Self when one receives the Divine hand of God over the heart. The heart resides in all creatures great and small, it is a tiny spec of awareness and yet its greatness supersedes all of existence. The heart of mankind can do justice by speaking to the hearts of all creatures and not just itself. Mankind is a tiny, fathomable entity just short of all creatures, it is no bigger or no smaller than any other creature God intended for this Divine leela. It is a sadness in the heart of God that oneness does not prevail, his intention was to see the beauty reflected back in all things, not just one. Humanity has lost its way, its navigator is off course and it would do well to remember that God is the creator, will always be the creator, and can only ever be the creator here on Earth.

Karma Yoga
REFLECTION

·Chapter III·

You, and everything that is, act like a mirror of Divine Consciousness.Until now you may not have realised this, but now you are realising your Divine Nature. See yourself in all, and all in your self. A reflection is whatever is looking back at you, whatever you perceive. Just as with a mirror, when you look into all of God's creation you will see your own Self reflected back. Creation is God's mirror, and you are God's reflection - God's perception is looking back at you.

Questions
1.Is the Atman hidden in the heart of all creatures?
2.What is Bhakti law?
3.How can you apply Bhakti law?
4.Is God holding your heart?
5.Can you accept all creatures great and small are the same as you?
6.Does the greatness of the heart supersede all of existence?
7.Do you believe mankind is equal in God's creation?
8.What is God's Divine leela?
9.How has humanity lost God's intention?
10.How can you get your navigator back on course?

Today: Remember as much as possible that everything that is and everything that will ever be was created in God's image. We all have the heart of God pumping love in our beings.Look around you in every moment see the hand of God at play, experience the heart of God in all that you see, feel and touch. Ask God as your creator to assist you to remember that you were created by him, for him and not for your own endeavours. Say to yourself often, 'God - your will not mine.'

Verse 21

Verse
'I know this undecaying, ancient, the soul of all, who is omnipresent on account of his all-pervading nature and whom the knowers of Brahman declare to be free from birth, whom the knowers of Brahman proclaim to be eternal.'

JnaniYoga
You are experiencing yourself as light now, you may move through all of creation. You may touch your consciousness wherever you will. There is nowhere you cannot go. Practice experiencing yourself as light. Look at a flam e, a fire, a light bulb, and imagine that you are like this light. Feel as though you can move through all of matter at will.

·Chapter III·

Keep a journal, a record of your experiences and develop belief in yourself as this light. Identify yourself as light. Wherever you see light, acknowledge yourself in the reflection.

Bhakti Yoga
I know that myself is free. I know that myself is love. I know that myself is eternal. I know that myself never ceases. I know that myself is myself. I know with all my heart and soul that I am the One True Creator, intrinsically bound to a Supreme Consciousness, so tightly woven into the fabric of my being that any attempts to deny myself are futile and unworthy of air. I know I can be at one with who I really am and make an everlasting truth become my very existence, my very reason for living, for life itself is of my own making. I can create, I am a worthy adversary for the darkness not to prevail. The light is so strong, so rich, so full inside my being. My consciousness is light, it's everywhere, it moves fluid through my being, through your being, through all beings. Like air it breathes its own breath, it is its own true reality - Brahman, Brahman, Brahman.

Karma Yoga
FLUIDITY
Fluidity is the capacity within to flow effortlessly, moving through, above, below, around,beyond all objects, all material-just as you hold a piece of paper against a light,and the light moves effortlessly through the paper.So too,do you move effortlessly through all things.Only your limited mind could lack belief in this Divine law.

Questions
1.What is omnipresent?
2.Who is free from birth?
3.Whom do the knowers of Brahman proclaim to be eternal?
4.Are you free?
5.Are you love? Do you know this to be true?
6.Are you bound to a Supreme Consciousness?
7.Do you create your own life?
8.Are you a worthy adversary for the darkness not to prevail?
9.Is your consciousness light?
10.Is this light of consciousness who you really are?

Today:Imagine that your consciousness is like light moving fluid through your being, through their being, through that being, through the being.Feel as though every breath you inhale and exhale is light.The light of love, the light of free, the highest eternal, the light of ceaseless existence, the light of your Self!

·Chapter III·

Main Point of Chapter III

THE RELATIONSHIP BETWEEN THE SENSES AND THE SELF

The main point being conveyed to you throughout Chapter III is about your relationship with your senses from the viewpoint of your SELF. The Self inside all beings must cultivate a deeper, more meaningful understanding of the senses and its relationship with the SELF for Self Realisation to deepen . This realisation starts with compassion, and an awareness of God's compassion for you.

a)Realise your humanity.
b)An awareness of sameness.
c)Knowingness.
d)Experience Truth.
e)Summon courage.
f)Realise your formless Self.
g)Liberate from seperative existence.
h)Manifest reality.
i)Learn patience.
j)Experience nothingness.
k)Generate light.
l)Cultivate your need for God.
m)Yearn for God.
n)Be more certain.
o)Reside in Samadhi.
p)Learn to be creative.
qFeel God's protection.
r)Express the senses of consciousness.
s)Share your Self with all you meet.
t)Experience yourself flowing effortlessly.

This Chapter outlines, and clearly guides you towards an ever greater experience of how to understand your senses and how to access your Divine senses. Therefore, altering your connection to an elevated state of consciousness; being all things Brahman intended you to be.

·Chapter IV·

Verse 1

Verse
'May that divine being, the one who, though himself colourless, creates various colours in different ways by means of his own power with self purpose and who dissolves the whole world in himself in the end - may he endow us with intellect.'

JnaniYoga
There are habits that form in the mind. They are old unwanted desires, behaviours, attachments. These vasanas are keeping you from God, but also bringing you closer to him. When you were a small child you experienced a desperate need inside, a need for love. This need was unmet; no human can satisfy this need in you. Only God can meet this fundamental need. You forgot your need was for God, and you transferred this genuine need onto those around you, in your immediate environment. You learnt from them how to relate to them, how to get your needs met from them. This is when your vasanas develop, which are an aspect of the karmic system. These behaviours become your 'game' to play, so you could (with desperation) join the game of life, whereby everyone behaves according to their vasanas to meet their needs. For example: A boy learns that when he is naughty he gets attention from his parents, so he grows up finding ways and means to get attention through being naughty. This is how he learnt to meet his need. But, when he realises his 'game' and desperately wants to receive God's love and attention, he relates to God from this mistaken belief; he acts 'naughty' with God to get

·Chapter IV·

attention. So, now you are ready to transform these vasanas into Divine behaviours , you need to behave how God intended. The boy becomes 'good' to get attention from God, and the more he behaves in this way, the more he connects with God, and the more he is motivated to change. Because the feelings you receive from loving God in this way far outweigh the painful feelings generated from acting upon your vasanas.

Bhakti Yoga

The many forms of God that live and breathe amongst the backdrop of life are without cause or meaning, they are the only obstacle to life itself. They are the colourless bone, sinew, muscles of karmic vasanas. They live lifeless, death has become them in the recesses of the tiny, shallow mine of the mind. They eat away at the consciousness of Self Realisation, believing themselves to be reality, they devour the light of knowledge day by day, week by week, month by month, year by year. They control our very movements away from the darkness and towards the light. They manip ulate, they lie. They make us feel whole and complete with their weight and heaviness. They are the constructs of an old mind, once real but never forgotten. They are the past, present, the future of our existence. The world comprises of them all, and yet there is no world with them. The basis of life is God, the basis of humanity is love, the basis of existence is to merge back with Supreme Consciousness, to realise the futility of holding onto a path tread with old shoes, old ways, old thinking.

Karma Yoga
VASANAS

Vasanas are old, unwanted, outdated attitudes and behaviours that have reincarnated with your form, and the process of Realisation is to let them go, to no longer identify with them. You must reach a place inside where you feel you do not want these anymore. Vasanas are painful, and keep you separate from God. They are an aspect of the karmic system, but are far more subtle, and insipid. You must practice asking God to meet your needs in positive, healthy ways.

Questions

1.What is intellect?
2.What are karmic vasanas?
3.Are you aware of your own personal vasanas?
4.How do your vasanas devour your knowledge?
5.How do vasanas control you?
7.How does the world comprise of vasanas?
8.How is there no world with vasanas?
9.What is the real basis of life?

·Chapter IV·

10.How do you let go of old habits?

Today: Let go of what no longer fits onto your path. Look around at your path now, what do you feel? Look in the mirror, what do you see? Look at yourself, what do you know about yourself now? Break away from old habits of thinking and feeling, let them go, breathe and absorb them back into Divine Consciousness. Let the light of love, the light of knowledge, remove them from view and see what is real, see what is true for you now. Be the change that you want to see in the world and the world will change right before you, it will transform into the reality of its existence - it exists to reabsorb your consciousness, to breakdown your old habits until all you are left with is all you can see, feel and know is you.

Verse 2

Verse
'That itself is Agni (fire), that is Aditya (the sun), that is Vayu (air), that is Chandrama (the moon), that is also the starry firmament, that is water, that is Prajapati.'

JnaniYoga
Identifying yourself with your vasanas will only serve to take you closer towards them. If you need to let go of your vasanas, you must focus on your Divine Nature. Our natural environment serves this purpose beautifully, God created nature and most is untainted by humankind. The environment in which we live is a perfect reflection of the Atman. It effortlessly serves God, without question, logic or reason. It just is what it is, and does what it was intended to do. Spend time in nature, go for a walk in the countryside. Breathe in the air, and allow this natural environment to remind you of your own True Nature.

Bhakti Yoga
Look around you, look at nature, there is always something natural everywhere you are to remind you of your own nature. A beautiful summer morning, a divine night sky, the air you breathe, the fire that makes you warm, the vastness of the ocean. Nature is a constant reflection of all that is beautiful, all that is wonderment, to inspire you to go inside to feel, to know the truth of who you are. All the various aspects of your one True Nature, all available in your outer environment. But, all available in your inner environment. Open your eyes, open your mind, open your heart, see with your inner eye the fire of your soul, the sun of your inner light shining bright, the air of your inner breath, your reflection of your inner moon at your third eye, the many myriads of Divine attributes - your inner

·Chapter IV·

stars. You are Brahman, you are Brahman, you are Brahman. See the water of yourself inside you reflected back by the supreme beauty of the natural environment. That is you, that is me. That is us, that is we.

Karma Yoga
NATURE
Nature is your intended state as ordained by the Divine. The earth, the trees, plants, flowers, water, sky etc are all manifestations of nature. Inside all beings is an essence of this nature. An intended state of being that feels comfortable, normal, natural to us when realised. We often work against our True Nature and this leaves us feeling uncomfortable, awkward and unnatural.

Questions
1.What is fire, the sun, air and the moon reflecting to you about yourself?
2.Do you spend time in nature?
3.How does nature remind you of yourself?
4.What do you feel when you spend time in nature?
5.How are you beautiful and breathtaking?
6.How can you be inspired to be more like nature?
7.Can you define the different aspects of nature - such as effortless etc?
8.How does your inner eye experience nature differently to your outer eyes?
9.What are your Divine attributes?
10.How can you maintain the memory of nature in daily life?

Today: Spend some time - stop whatever you are doing, and go inside. See with you inner eye the beauty of your natural inner environment. The air, the fire, the light, the water. If you notice anything unnatural to you such as thoughts, feelings, desires, notice how unnatural they feel now that you are focusing your attention on your supreme natural environment. Keep the memory throughout the day and whenever you feel lost or confused about who you are just close your eyes and go back inside and be at one with your One True Nature, Brahman, Brahman, Brahman.

Verse 3

Verse
'Thou art the woman, thou art the man, thou art the youth, thou art the maiden too, thou art the old man who totters along leaning on the staff, thou art born with thy face turned everywhere.'

·Chapter IV·

JnaniYoga
How can you see yourself as a tree? If you look, observe and witness your form, can you experience your form as you would a tree? Can you allow your form to remind you of what it is that has manifested as form? Everything that you are is inside the form of yourself. Practice seeing your Atman through your form. Don't ignore the form , or discount it. Use it to see who you are. Alter your perception, look at your physical body as you would look at a tree.

Bhakti Yoga
Man, woman and child. Trees, rivers, plants and minerals, animals, insects, birds and bees all wear the face of Brahman. When you look around you the face of God smiles back from wherever you can see with your Brahman eyes. Your eyes, ears, nose, hands and mouth bear the mark of Brahman. You know you are seeing like Brahman when all you can see is beauty. You know you are hearing Brahman when all you can hear is melody. You know you are smelling Brahman when all you can smell is sweet. You know when you are touching Brahman when all you can touch is soft. You know when you are tasting Brahman when all you can taste is amrita - the divine nectar. Everything, everywhere, at all times carries the mark of the Divine hand of beauty, melody, sweetness, softness and amrita - the divine nectar.

Karma Yoga
AMRITA
Amrita is a Sanskrit word that literally means immortality and is often referred to as nectar. Amrita is an energy provided by God which you can actually taste whilst in the experience of it. It is a fluid that flows from your pituary gland down the throat in deep states of meditation. It tastes sweet like honey, and is the product of living life according to God's will.

Questions
1.Why do we have form in our physical manifestation?
2.What does it mean to be a man, woman or child?
3.How can you see your form as God intended?
4.Can you see Brahman in your form?
5.Do you see Brahman in all forms?
6.Do you see the beauty of all in God's forms?
7.Do you hear melody in all things? Do you smell sweetness in all things? Do you touch softness in all things? Do you taste Amrita in all things?
8.What is Amrita?
9.Have you ever been affected by Amrita?
10.How can you taste life according to God's will?

·Chapter IV·

Today: When you see something, see past the form and see its beauty. When you hear something, see past its form and hear the melody. When you smell something, see past its form and smell its sweetness. When you touch something, see past its form and feel its softness. When you taste something see past its form and taste Amrita - the Divine nectar.

Verse 4

Verse
'Thou art the dark blue fly. Thou art the green parrot with red eyes. Thou art the thunder-cloud, the seasons and the oceans. Thou art without beginning, thou art the infinite. Thou art he from whom all the worlds are born.'

JnaniYoga
Living life according to God's will, seeing the beauty in all things. Being in an experience of awe and wonderment at the magnificent sight of all that is, and all that will ever be. Hold the idea of this magnificent journey within your being for as long as possible, as often as possible throughout the day.

Bhakti Yoga
All the worlds are born free, a spirit lives within them all, colourful, beautiful, radiant, awe inspiring. A beauty second to none. A spirit that can soar through every world, that can destroy every living thing, that can change at any given moment and that will reflect a magnificent hue of effervescent glory. It is immeasurable, it cannot be quantified, there are no vessels large enough to hold it. It is a seamless reality no more, no less. It gives birth to all of creation, the creation of you.

Karma Yoga
RADIANCE
Life emits an energy of a sublime nature. This energy is radiance. A view of the world as shining brightly, like everything is light, and alive.

Questions
1.How do the words, 'Thou art,' make you feel?
2.Are you without beginning, and infinite?
3.Are you the 'he' from whom all the worlds are born?
4.What does it mean: 'The worlds are born free'?
5.Do you experience the spirit living within the world?
6.Are you awe inspired by the world?

·Chapter IV·

7.How does the spirit soar through every world?
8.Is the spirit immeasurable?
9.Can you quantify spirit?
10.Do you see yourself in the vastness of creation?

Today: See yourself in the vastness of all of creation.

Verse 5

Verse
'There is one unborn being, a female of red, white and black colours who produces many offsprings like herself. There is one unborn being, male, who loves her and lies by her, there is another unborn male who leaves her after having enjoyed her.'

JnaniYoga
Push, push yourself. Allow others to push you, challenge you, pull you out of your comfort zone. Read, study, worship, act, feel, think, do something daily to move the obstacles of lethargy. Don't allow yourself to stay comfortable. You are going to have to push, you are over half way now, and it's getting harder. You need to be more serious, more focused, more willing to be uncomfortable.

Bhakti Yoga
Nature in all her unborn beauty is Shakti, the powerful, unawakened creative ability to push, to pull, to rest awhile. The cycle of unconscious, unmet needs of creation willing itself to be made manifest. To experience the experiencer in all of God's creation. To manifest the unmanifest, like a tiny seed resting, sleeping, feeding, patiently in the ground of life. Needing water, sun, to awaken from its restful sleep. To feed diligently so it can push itself up out of the ground to experience the beauty, the One True Nature of itself. To awaken to its Real Nature, its Divine calling. Then there is another that feeds off the nature of God to fulfil its all selfish, all self centred desires. Its will to manifest its own wishes, to fulfil its own dreams. It lies dormant in the ground, never reaching up, never pushing itself away from the darkness towards the light. It dies in the ground, lifeless, dull, ceasing to exist, resting permanently without cause, without purpose, without experiencing its one true purpose, its Divine creative task to experience itself for God.

Karma Yoga
SHAKTI
She is a fierce, warrior like energy that is the female version of the Divine.

·Chapter IV·

She forces you to grow, to learn, to push when you go slow. She is very powerful, and will not take no for an answer. Shakti loves you by challenging you to be greater. She does not give in to your lower nature, and forces you to pull yourself out of any negative behaviours. She does not allow you to waste any time , and drives you towards Realisations with her strong will.

Questions
1.What is Shakti?
2.How do you experience Shakti?
3.How does Shakti push you to manifest?
4.How are you creative with your spiritual practice?
5.What are your unconscious , unmet needs?
6.Do you have a strong will?
7.How do you cultivate the energy of Shakti?
8.How are you lazy, selfish and self centred?
9.What does it feel like to give in to your self-centred nature?
10.What action are you going to take to experience more Shakti in daily life?

Today: Think about how you are pushing yourself out of the darkness towards the light. Think about how you are meeting God's needs for you, and how you are selfishly meeting your own.

Verse 6

Verse
'Two birds of beautiful plumage, who are inseparable friends, dwell upon one and the same tree. Of these two the one eats the sweet fruit, while the other looks on without eating.'

JnaniYoga
Go deeper, build more of a relationship with God. All relationships require effort, regardless of the nature of the relationship. There are basic rules, principles that apply to all relationships. If you seek to have a strong relationship with God, do not rely upon God to do all the hard work. Work hard to cultivate a relationship, get to know him/her, be honest with God about yourself, let God into your inner world, consciously develop an awareness of this relationship. Talk to him, listen to him, communicate your hopes, dreams, fears , doubts etc.

Bhakti Yoga
The Supreme Consciousness and the Individual Consciousness are one and the

same thing. Trying to separate them is likened to attempting to separate a wave in the ocean from the ocean itself. Just as an individual wave cannot be separated from the vast ocean, a Jiva cannot be separated from the Lord. But, you will witness a wave appear to be separating itself from the ocean as it is forced up by the powers of nature. Likewise, the Jiva is powerless against the force of the powers of desire for sensory pleasures. These desires force the Jiva further away from its connection to the Lord, and closer to separation. It is in separation from our True Nature that we experience the most pain. We forget, just like the birds who are inseparable friends, that ourself and the Lord are inseparable friends - sitting together on the tree of life.

Karma Yoga
JIVA
Jiva means Individual. I am separate, there is a part of me that is unique, not the same. It is defined by my identity, my personal identification with my chosen God. Being an individual enables you to relate to God better, and also supports you in bringing your own needs to God, rather than the needs of others. Identifying your Jiva enables you to build a strong and honest relationship with God. You share with God your individuality and he responds to you personally.

Questions
1.What is Jiva?
2.How are you an individual?
3.What distracts you from being an individual?
4.Do you ever feel afraid of being separate, unique?
5.Can you believe the Supreme and Individual consciousness are one and the same?
6.Do you know that you cannot be truly separated from the Lord?
7.Do you feel separate from God?
8.Are you powerless against your desires?
9.How do your desires force you away from God?
10.How can you and the Lord be inseparable friends?

Today: Imagine you are inseparable friends with the Lord, sitting together on the tree of life. Think about the qualities of a true friend, such as loyalty, care, trust etc and cultivate these qualities in your relationship with God.

Verse 7

Verse
'Dwelling on the same tree, the Individual Soul gets entangled and feels

·Chapter IV·

miserable. He is deluded and grieves for his impotence. When he sees the other, the Lord, contented and knows his glory, he becomes freed from sorrow.'

JnaniYoga
This journey can feel like a roller coaster ride, and at this point you are probably thinking that you would like some stability, some consistent contentment. The journey itself isn't actually designed to be like a roller coaster ride, up and down, never on level ground. God designed the journey to be level, and from a higher perception you can see that it is. The cause of this feeling of up and down comes from your inner turmoil, and a lack of faith. With faith you can experience ups and downs, but you do not feel any discomfort, you just relax and enjoy the ride. It is this state of relaxation that makes the journey feel level, and grounded. Practice relaxing, and trusting more that even though you are still travelling, the journey is being navigated by God, all is perfect, all is well.

Bhakti Yoga
The Individual Soul desires, he desires objects, he lusts after greedy, wilful wants and likes, he becomes entangled with his mind of wanton desires. He wants this and that, that and this. He becomes caught up in the need for glory, for power, for personal gain. He no longer sees beauty in the world reflected back at him, but anger, lust, fear, greed - he hates his life, but he wants so much that he negates his real nature and the truth. He has lost his sense of freedom and wants to get off the tree, to venture out alone in the sea of darkness. He no longer knows who he is, or no longer wishes to know. Only when he sees the vision of the Lord sat peacefully and content in all his glory does he begin to realise the error of his ways. He then knows, and believes there is another way to be, to know that faith and focus on the Lord will surely bring that to me. But, first he has to want that, and not this. He has to want to be freed from his sorrowful desires that entangle him in pain and suffering. He has to desire God.

Karma Yoga
DISCERNMENT
Knowing the difference between two or more things. It is important to be able to see that God does not have vasanas, he is content always. There is a part of you also, like God, that does not have vasanas and is content. But, when your vasanas are controlling you, you need to be able to tell the difference. You need to be able to recognise that your vasanas are not God. If you do not practice this, you can very easily get lost, and lose your way for longer than necessary. The power within to be able to tell the difference between what is real and what is unreal is discernment.

·Chapter IV·

Questions

1.Do you feel miserable when your Individual Soul gets entangled?
2.How do you become deluded and grieve for your impotence?
3.How do you see God in these times?
4.Does seeing God contented free you from this sorrow?
5.What do you 'want'?
6.How do you get caught up in your own personal life again?
7.Do you ever hate life?
8.What is it like when you completely lose all knowledge of yourself?
9.How do you cultivate faith?
10.How can you desire God?

Today: Pray: 'God give me the strength, the courage, the wisdom to be content sitting restfully with you on the tree of life. Give me the power of discernment to know the difference between my desire for God, for truth, and my desire for material objects. Let me surrender to my essential need for you above all else, I need you, I need you, I need you.'

Verse 8

Verse

'Of what use are the Vedas to him who does not know that indestructible, highest ethereal being in whom all the Gods and the Vedas reside? Only those who know that, rest contented.'

JnaniYoga

A solid, structured, guaranteed way of understanding God is experiencing God inside through knowledge of the Self. It is possible to read every book, study every scripture, analyse every text known to man. But, unless you have direct experience of the Self and knowledge from within pours forth, the study of books is futile and a waste of time. God cannot be known by mere intellect alone, logic and reason constitute only a small part of this journey. The unexplainable, the times in your life when you feel as though you are directly experiencing God are invaluable. Study, learn, explore, but then allow time for the experience to rise up from within and let it be known.

Bhakti Yoga

Know me for I am you. I am you today. I am you tomorrow. I am you all your yesterdays. I am freedom. I am knowledge. I am love. I am desireless. I am you. God cannot be known by any other name than his own name. God cannot be known through books or bookish knowledge. God can only be known through

·Chapter IV·

knowledge of the Self. Knowledge of the Self alone gives you a direct experience of the Divine. Inner knowledge comes from direct experience of the unexplainable. The touch that cannot be felt, the vision that cannot be described, the sound that cannot be heard.

Karma Yoga
UNEXPLAINABLE
Having a solid, profound experience which logic and reason cannot describe, or understand, how it could be possible . This is the meaning of unexplainable. It is an absolute fact that everyone has had experiences in their life that they cannot possibly explain, but that they know with all certainty are true. This is a time to loosen your grip on logic, and allow for the wonderment of the illogical to manifest.

Questions
1.What are the Vedas?
2.'God is an indestructible, high ethereal being.' Explain what this means to you.
3.Do you feel contentment when you relax and do not hold onto book knowledge?
4.What is the difference between book knowledge, and knowledge of the Self?
5.Do you ever experience book knowledge?
6.Do you value knowledge of the Self over book knowledge?
7.Do you agree that when you know God, you know yourself more?
8.What are direct experiences of the Divine? 9. What is unexplainable?
10.Think about the experiences you have had that you cannot explain.

Today: Feel what you cannot explain, see what you cannot describe, hear what cannot be heard. And know you are at one in that ve,y moment with the Divine.

Verse 9

Verse
'The Lord of Maya projects or creates the Vedas, the sacrifices, the ceremonies, religious observances, what has been, what is to be, all that the Vedas declare and this whole world, including ourselves. The other is bound by Maya in this.'

JnaniYoga
Life truly is a reflection of all that you are inside. Your perception of the world, of your own unique life guides you, directs you, ushers you forward. It matters how you see these things because your perception now affects your present choices, and your present choices will decide your future. So, it really matters how you

·Chapter IV·

perceive the world, and your life. If you see the world as dark and miserable, you will create more of this in your life. If you see the world as full of beauty, you will create more beauty in your life. Make a conscious decision today to see things as they are. Practice adjusting your perception, so that what you see is who you really are, and not the old, outdated version of yourself.

Bhakti Yoga
God has created a beautiful world for us to play and learn, to laugh and be free. A world full of beauty, wonderment and awe. A world so perfect that only God could be seen, felt and heard. And yet, our limited selves view this world as a prison - a dark, dull, lifeless entity full of traps and poisons, pain and suffering. Only the mind of an Enlightened Being can truly know what is real in this creative flow of life force energy. Listen to the Great Masters, feel how they radiate the essence of the True Intention of God, the way they describe the natural beauty of the world God intended for us. Only the mind of a soul in bondage can truly see something else, only that mind can see the illusion of an unreal reality - one of darkness and pain. Only an unrealised soul can see its self reflected back, only an unrealised soul can see its own dark corners in the corners of the world.

Karma Yoga
GREAT MASTERS
The Great Masters look like you, may act like you, dress like you etc. But they have a noticeable difference. They know they are in the world, but not of the world. They can distinguish between the real and the unreal. They know with all certainty the Art of Being God. They do not learn about God, study, think or feel about God. They are a living God.

Questions
1.What does it mean to project?
2.Do the Vedas, sacrifices, ceremonies and religious observances benefit you?
3.Do you ever play, laugh and be free?
4.Are you always extremely serious?
5.Is the world perfect to you?
6.Do you see misery in the world?
7.How do you alter your perception to be more Divine?
8.Do you know the difference between projecting your real Self, and your old self onto the world?
9.How can you practice projecting your real Self onto the world?
10.Do you realise everything you see is inside you?

Today: Be objective with yourself. Stop what you are doing and look around

·Chapter IV·

your environment, look at the world God created for you. What do you see? If you see darkness - realise the darkness is inside you. If you see misery - realise the misery is inside you. If you see beauty - realise the beauty is inside you. If you see wonderment - realise the wonderment is inside you. Choose to see yourself as God intended. See beyond the darkness and misery - see the beauty, be in awe of yourself!

Verse 10

Verse
'Know that prakriti (nature) is maya, and the great God is the Lord of maya. This whole world is pervaded by beings who are his parts.'

JnaniYoga
Can you imagine yourself as an actor, playing a role in a play or film? The character you have been given to play is your karma, and the director is God. Are you a good actor? Do you identify with your character, and play your role to the best of your ability? Are you easy to direct, or are you a primadonna, wanting to control things to go your way? Practice being in the film of your life. See yourself in the main role, learn your lines well, understand the character you are playing.

Bhakti Yoga
All of nature, everything around us, everything natural is governed and controlled by God. Every person is a part of nature, a part of this natural world, a part of God. We are all governed and directed by a powerful, natural Divine force that leads us out of darkness of unawareness towards the light of realisation. There is no corner, no place in the entire universe that is not governed by God. Know that there is no place to hide where God cannot find you and lead you towards realising the truth of who you are - leading you away from the illusion that you are in some way separate from this Divine play (leela). The part you play, the script you read, the companions you act with, are all under the direction of the Lord. The spell of maya cast upon you is the goal, God will direct you away from the spell of disillusionment towards the path of Enlightenment.

Karma Yoga
MAYA
Maya is an illusion. Similar to the idea that when a rope is laid on the ground, it can be mistaken to be a snake. And, even though it is a rope, the belief that it is a snake will generate the same amount of panic and fear as a real snake would. This is the reality of the world. Your mind can perceive the unreal to be real and tell you to feel and respond exactly as you would as if it were real.

·Chapter IV·

Questions

1.What is Maya?
2.How is the world an illusion?
3.Do you know that when you look at a person and see a person , that you are actually seeing a snake? And, that you are actually a rope? And that metaphorical rope is God?
4.How is the world like a film/movie?
5.What character do you portray?
6.How do you approach your script?
7.How do you relate to your director?
8.Are you under the spell of disillusionment?
9.What is a Divine leela?
10.What is the path of Enlightenment?

Today: Close your eyes, hold out your hand and feel God take your hand and lead you towards your path, your path of Enlightenment.

Verse 11

Verse

'One attains infinite peace when he realises that Lord, the adorable God, the bestower of blessings who, though one, presides over the various aspects of prakriti and in whom this universe dissolves and in whom it appears in various forms.'

JnaniYoga

It is time to contemplate the role of the Guru for Self Realisation. It is my belief that the Upanishads are quite emphatically stating the absolute need for a Guru. And, in my experience the Guru makes the difference. Guru is Lord, Guru is a reflection of your Divinity in human form, Guru reminds you that you are God. There are so many Gurus to choose from, and it is said that the Guru chooses you. But, it is advisable now to explore the meaning of Guru, the various Guru's available and to practice following a Guru's direction.

Bhakti Yoga

The Guru is Lord, the Guru is known and unknown, the Guru is light and the Guru shares this light. The Guru awakens one to the realisation that all is a part of an indivisible soul. All is one and the same. Nothing is separate, nothing cannot be experienced by the whole. I am that that I am at all times, in all places, everywhere. The Guru resides over the whole universe breathing life into his parts. The parts are man walking the earth searching for the One, the whole

·Chapter IV·

searching to know itself around and around it goes. Where did I come from? Who am I to know? What purpose can I serve? Who am I? I am a part of a whole. The whole is the Lord. The hands are us, the feet are us, the body is us. Walk with me and know that I am you. Feel with me and know that I am you. Be with me and know that I am you. You produce life for me, you produce breath for me, you produce time for me, you produce all things at all times for me. I am the director of your play, and you are the producer of its parts. Together we achieve greatness. Together we experience a whole.

Karma Yoga
GURU

What is a Guru really? Who is a Guru? There are so many false Gurus, and so many people using the term Guru to refer to a teacher of some worldly matter - a fashion Guru etc. Guru means one who can take you from darkness to light. A Guru shows you the light, and works on so many different levels to draw you out of the darkness of ignorance, and into the light of knowledge. A True Guru is a Knower of Brahman, and if you ask them any question, will know with all certainty the answer. They will also emit light towards you, and this light will illuminate the Self within all, showing you who you really are. You will actually feel Divine in the presence of a Guru.

Questions

1.'A Guru can help you to understand God, and assist you in building a relationship with God.' Do you believe this to be true?
2.The last verse of Chapter VI in the Svetasvatara Upanishad states that you must have as much devotion to Guru as to God. How do you feel about this statement?
3.Do you have a Guru?
4.'The Guru is Lord.' What does this mean?
5.'The Guru is light.' How does a Guru share his light?
6.How does a Guru awaken you?
7.If you spoke to a Guru in this moment, what would you say/ask?
8.'A Guru produces experiences for you to grow and to learn that you could not produce yourself.' Explain what this means.
9.Can you work together with a Guru, or do you like to work alone?
10.Why would you slow the process of Realisation down by not having a Guru?

Today: Remember always that everything you produce - thoughts, feelings, actions, awarenesses are produced for me, with me and with me in mind.

·Chapter IV·

Verse 12

Verse

'May Audra, the Creator and Supporter of the Gods, the great Seer, the Lord of all, who saw Hiranyagobha being born, endow us with pure or auspicious intellect.'

JnaniYoga

Whilst building a relationship with God, it is advised that one uses a Guru to aid this, and speed this process up. It is far easier to relate to God in human form, than to attempt to know Brahman himself directly. Feelings of inadequacy and a lack of knowledge will inevitably stand in your way. Humility is required to surrender to a Guru, and humbly seek their direction and guidance. An individual can become so easily lost, and caught up in their vasanas. The Guru reminds you always of the light.

Bhakti Yoga

Strong, capable, powerful Lord - Lord God Almighty. Who has the power to destroy all three worlds, and still exist for thy devotees. Thy devotees bow to you Lord, thy devotees beg to you Lord, thy devotees cry in pain and misery, oh Lord, our Saviour Supreme. Break the shackles of denial, suffering and bondage. Break us free to walk in your light. To talk of your light. To share of your magnificent Self. How beautiful you are to us. Nothing of such beauty have we ever seen or will we ever see again. To walk where you have walked, oh what a thing of beauty, words can no longer be spoken of such greatness. Mere thoughts on a page do no justice to your splendour. May we beg your forgiveness for all our failings, our arrogance, our ignorance. We love you, we will always love you, we are in love with you.

Karma Yoga

DEVOTEE

A Guru is an advanced reflection of nature. First, we begin with our natural environment, seeing ourselves reflected back through trees, countryside, lakes and streams etc. But, then we must progress if we wish to advance further on our path. A Guru works just like nature, but the reflections are far more advanced. A devotee is one amongst us who can surrender control, and give their Self Realisation journey, lessons and results to the Guru. A devotee is one who can love the Guru, and in loving the Guru receive their enormous boons and Grace. A devotee must be able to accept the pace the Guru sets for their realisations. Having a guru makes Self Realisation fast, lessons more frequent and experiences of love profound and transformational.

·Chapter IV·

Questions

1.What is a devotee?
2.Could you be a devotee?
3.What are you devoted to now and how does this devotion affect you?
4.Do you beg for help?
5.Do you want to speed up your process of Realisation?
6.What are your fears about being a devotee?
7.Do you like to be in complete control?
8.How do you surrender your will?
9.A Guru has succeeded at Self Realisation, either in this life or another. Does that not excite you, and give you hope?
10.What kind of devotee would you be? The Bhakti sutras state that one can either be a servant, friend, child, parent, philosopher or spouse of the Divine.

Today: Bow down and beg for mercy from the Magnificent Creator of all that is and all that will ever be. Surrender your intellect and all that resides within your mind!

Verse 13

Verse

'Let us give reverence with oblations to that blissful God, who is the Lord of the Devas, who rules the bipeds and the quadrupeds and in whom all the worlds rest.'

JnaniYoga

Be open to receiving love. Open your heart, your mind and your body to the opportunity of love. God's love is very powerful and when experienced transforms you. Other forms of love will never satisfy you again once you have fully experienced the love of God. Make your being a vessel for God's love. Clean your cup to allow the water of Divine love to flow into it. Evaluate your eating and drinking habits, your relationships, your physical exercise, the environments you visit etc. Clean your house, both within and without. The cleaner you are, the more of a vessel you are.

Bhakti Yoga

I am the One, the Lord of Supreme Reality. Bow your being down in reverence and respect to my splendour, my magnificence. I am in you, in tiny droplets. Within your mind, within your body, within your heart. You can feel me when you are asleep, you can know me when you are awake. I am that soulful voice within that beckons you away from ignorance towards Enlightenment. I call out your name, I call out to

·Chapter IV·

you, 'Hear me, Hear me, Hear me,' I say, 'You are no longer alone. Lay down your being with me. Rest awhile in my peaceful embrace.'

Karma Yoga
BLISS
Bliss is the energy of Divine love. Bliss eliminates your thoughts, opens your heart, cleans your body, awakens knowledge and connects you with God.

Questions
1.Are you open to receiving love?
2.What is the difference between God's love and other forms of love?
3.How do you relate to your body as a vessel for God's love?
4.What are your eating habits?
5.Are you conscious when it comes to keeping your house clean, both within and without?
6.Have you ever experienced bliss?
7.Can you see how toxins can prevent you from experiencing bliss?
8.Do you revere the source of bliss?
9.Are you respectful towards God?
10.What can you do today to maintain a clean home?

Today: Open your mind, your body and your heart to the one true beauty of this world - bliss. Experience bliss in all that you do, say and be. Open your heart and see me there resting quietly in my home.

Verse 14

Verse
'He who realises him, who is subtler than the subtlest, who creates the world in the midst of chaos, who assumes many forms, who is the only one that envelops the world, the blissful one (Siva), attains infinite peace.'

JnaniYoga
Shiva is consciousness, and consciousness is Shiva. To be in love with Shiva is to be in love with consciousness. Consciousness is so complex, and words can never really describe it. But, in order to attempt at explaining consciousness one must break it down into differing aspects. Even though this is not completely accurate, it is also accurate. Such is the nature of consciousness. Consciousness is opposites, both hot and cold are consciousness. An attempt to make consciousness more obtainable follows... The process of Self Realisation is to move through these stages of consciousness:

·Chapter IV·

Ego.Consciousness - the need for something other than God.
Divine Consciousness - the realisation of the possibility of God being all encompassing, infinite and beyond measure.
Self Consciousness - the idea and belief that God is all there is, there is nothing in existence other than God.
Realisation - the consciousness of all no longer exists, there are no levels or awareness, only nothing is real.
Supreme Consciousness - the Supreme Being that all others are only servants of God, doing God's will, doing God's work, doing God's plan.
Everything in the universe fits into one of these stages.

Bhakti Yoga
Self Realisation is a stage of life, a stage of a soul's journey to oneness. It is not the final stage, it is the beginning. When a soul reaches maturity, it brings with it, into this life, a myriad of differing levels of consciousness to realise. One is Ego Consciousness - the need for something other than God. One is Divine Consciousness - the realisation of the possibility of God being all encompassing, infinite and beyond measure. One is Self Consciousness - the idea and belief that God is all there is, there is nothing in existence other than God. One is Realisation - the consciousness of all no longer exists there are no levels, or awareness, only nothing is real. And, one is Supreme Consciousness - the Supreme Being that all others are only servants of God, doing God's will, doing God's work, doing God's plan. When all beings realise that there is only God's plan, then there will be peace on earth. There will be peace inside all, peace inside everything and peace everywhere. This peace cannot be felt, thought, generated or experienced in any of the four preceding levels without the need for an external source of Supreme Consciousness. Supreme Consciousness is the power generated by God for his devotees to help them journey through the four levels. The only way to experience Supreme Consciousness alone is without form. Only a Guru can generate this kind of power source, only a Guru can plug into and merge with this Supreme Energy. A Guru does this by will, they can will themselves into existence to serve God in this way. And in this form their formed and formless Self vibrates at a level beyond the four levels, unexplainable, incomprehensible and absolutely nothing compares, nothing contrasts, nothing comes close to this experience. Nothing.

Karma Yoga
SHIVA
Shiva is a warrior and peaceful. A husband and an ascetic. Shiva is loving and ferocious. Shiva is everything, and Shiva is nothing. Shiva is consciousness.

·Chapter IV·

Questions
1.What is Shiva?
2.How is Shiva consciousness?
3.Do you understand the stages of consciousness?
4.Can you see that you experience all five stages at different times?
5.Is there one particular stage of consciousness that you prefer?
6.Can you see now that Self Realisation also is only a stage in life?
7.How do you feel that Self Realisation is only the beginning?
8.Can you imagine a world where everyone realises there is only God's plan?
9.Do you strive for peace?
10.Have you observed a transformation in your own consciousness in the moment it occurs?

Today: Try to experience the vibration of a Guru - be in their presence and experience a transformation in your own consciousness. Whilst in their presence you will reach higher and higher states.

Verse 15

Verse
'He alone is the protector of the world at the proper time. He is the Lord of all the world hidden in all beings. In him the Brahma-rishis and the deities merge themselves. He who knows him thus, cuts asunder the fetters of death.'

JnaniYoga
Direct your own experience, create situations where you can feel the Divine. Don't just read this book, go out into the world and merge with everything you encounter. Live life to its fullest, meet new people, make new friends, join groups, share your knowledge, go to new places, live.

Bhakti Yoga
Guru, God, Shiva, Brahman, Oneness, words , concepts , ideas, beliefs, philosophies . Of what use are these without meaning, without direct experience of Him? And who is he, can he ever be experienced, will he ever be known? Can I know him? It is true that these ideas can free your mind from control, but what can free your mind from the ideas? The ideas themselves are held, are known, and yet still are limiting. Limiting ideas generate fear ever still, more and more fear. This fear, it suffocates and restricts the breath of knowing. Remove the fear with love, only love. But then what is love, and how can love be known with all these limiting ideas?

·Chapter IV·

Love has the power to dissolve all ideas, and leave you with the mind that no ideas existed at all.

Karma Yoga
EXPERIENCE
Experience is when you let life happen to you, you relinquish control of life. Every moment is an opportunity, a new chance for adventure, for excitement. There are endless possibilities. The fullness and richness of life awaits you.

Questions
1.Do you experience life?
2.Are you controlling?
3.How easy do you find it to let go and live?
4.Do you create new adventures?
5.How often do you meet new people?
6.Do you ever share your knowledge with others?
7.How do you feel when you let life happen by itself?
8.What is the difference between living and surviving?
9.What are you experiencing right now in your life?
10.How does God direct your experiences?

Today: Face fear head on and pray for it to stop existing.

Verse 16

Verse
'He who knows Siva, the blissful one, who is hidden in all beings in an extremely subtle form, finer than the essence of ghee, who alone envelops the universe, is freed from all fetters.'

JnaniYoga
Free yourself from old patterns, old ways of thinking. Try new inner experiences. You have tasted the adventure of living life, and letting it happen. Now, try this in your inner world. Let your mind wander wherever it must go, don't control it. Let your emotions flow without restriction. Allow yourself an inner adventure. Give yourself time throughout the day to just wander inwardly wherever you must go.

Bhakti Yoga
The chatter, the minds continuous gaze ever filling itself up on mindless attachments, darkness and the cold. Oh the cold, it envelops my being and takes hold and won't let go. But let go it must. It must allow me the light of your warmth,

·Chapter IV·

your ever blissfulness in me must awaken me from this blinding fear that disables me from moving forward. But move forward I must now, I must move forward. Let me go, hold out no more, free me from your unenlightenment, free me from your unenlightenment, free me from your unenlightenment.

Karma Yoga
RELEASE
Everyone has a tight hold, a strong grip on what they will allow themselves to experience. Release happens when you loosen your grip, your hold on attachments.

Questions
1.Does your mind chatter incessantly?
2.Do you attach yourself to your thoughts?
3.Do you believe everything your mind tells you?
4.Can your mind fill up with darkness?
5.Is your mind ever cold?
6.Does your mind generate a lot of fear?
7.How do you release yourself from your thoughts?
8.How does Enlightenment relate to thoughts?
9.Can you imagine loving your thoughts?
10.Do you experience your thoughts dissolving as they experience love?

Today: Remove yourself from your unenlightened state. Release yourself from the grip of attachment and experience my blissful love enveloping thee.

Verse 17

Verse
'That God, the creator of the universe, the supreme soul, always dwells in the hearts of all beings, being limited by the heart, intellect and mind.
Those who know this become immortal.'

JnaniYoga
The time has come to reflect on all you have learnt thus far. Go back over your answers to all the previous lessons, and reflect on where you have been, where you are now, and where you are reaching towards. Read through your responses, and then relax. Spend some time in deep reflection; meditate on who you have become. Then, when you are ready, use the awareness of your growth to push you on, to continue steadfast on this your journey of transformation.Believe in yourself, and have faith that you are nearly two thirds of the way home.

·Chapter IV·

Bhakti Yoga
My heart is filled with heaviness. I can no longer go on. I feel unworthy of your knowledge, I feel bound, trapped in an ever limiting cycle of bondage and hopelessness. I must muster up all that I have become and move ever further still. I must continue, I must push on, I must move myself out of your way and let your love shine through me, with me, in me, as me.

Karma Yoga
PUSH
It's getting harder now, the challenge is more real. Everything of value is worth fighting for. To push means to fight, to remove all obstacles ahead with a mighty force of will. Will yourself forward, don't give up, continue, focus, strive for Truth. Truth alone can set you free. Seek this freedom with every ounce of your being.

Questions
1.What does it mean to reflect on where you have been?
2.How do you feel about where you used to be?
3.How much have you changed?
4.Do you believe in yourself more now?
5.How has your faith in God grown?
6.Do you experience a heaviness in your heart?
7.Do you ever feel like giving up?
8.Are you unworthy of knowledge?
9.What can you do when you experience helplessness?
10.How can you push yourself on?

Today: Know that there is more still to move, to push, to pull. Don't give up. Don't give in to hopelessness. Continue, continue, continue.

Verse 18

Verse
'When ignorance has disappeared, then there is neither day or night, neither existence nor no existence. Then there is only Siva, the all-blessed one, who is imperishable, the adorable light of Savita (the deity of the sun). From him the ancient wisdom has proceeded.'

JnaniYoga
You want God now, you are frustrated with yourself, and also with God. Impatience has become normal, there is a relentless feeling of discontent in your being, more often than you would like. The only way to combat this discontentment is to be

completely driven with an absolute lust for the Divine. Tell God how desperate you are. Get down on your knees and beg for mercy upon your soul. Throw yourself at the feet of God, and cry, wail, pray for strength and courage, the will to pick yourself up, and with outstretched arms reach for more and more God.

Bhakti Yoga
I am pushing, and yet confusion is filling my mind. Am I not enough, am I not there? Is the here I am journeying towards not to be reached? I must prevail I must conquer I must succeed. I cannot be pulled away by mere attachments, by noises in my mind. These noises are without reason for me now, I no longer desire them, the desire for them left me long ago. And yet still I can't breathe without them, they are still the cause of such pain in me. I need them no more, I want for them no more, I cannot go on for a moment with the unrealistic idea of them still implanted in my mind. Leave now, you are free to journey on without me, you are free to continue ahead without me, you are free to forge a path without me.

Karma Yoga
DESIRE
I have got to have it, and I will do anything to get it. This is desire. It is uncontrollable, insatiable, enveloping. It completely takes over, nothing else matters but the object of your desire.

Questions
1.Look at how far you have come that you want God so badly. How does it feel to have reached this place?
2.Why do you get confused?
3.What happens when you feel like you're not enough?
4.Do you despair when you feel you can't reach your destination?
5.Are you determined to succeed?
6.Do you feel contempt towards your attachments?
7.Do you still desire a noisy mind?
8.Are you firm with your desires? 9. Do you only desire God?
10. What energy do you put into desiring God?

Today: Know that when the end is in sight you will falter but you must pick yourself up and carry on seemingly without me.

Verse 19

Verse
'No one can grasp him above, or across, or in the middle. There is no

·Chapter IV·

likeness (or equal) of him whose name is great glory.'

JnaniYoga
You have to accept that no matter what you do, no matter how far you reach there will always be more to know, to strive, to reach towards . You need to accept that there is no final destination. You are reaching for a place that does not exist. This is the time for contemplation, and relaxation. Contemplate the idea that there is no end, this is an endless journey, the more you know, the less you know. Emptying yourself of all mistaken beliefs leaves you with Nothing. And in that state of nothingness you know everything, but consciously you have no awareness of thoughts, you will experience abundance, and lack at the same time.

Bhakti Yoga
I am a tiny spec of dust in the vast desert of your Divine will. I will always know you, and even when I do not know your name, I will always know you. I can never not know you. In all the planes of existence I will know you. In all the realities of consciousness I will always know you. You are to be known and yet I will never know you. You are a contradiction to me. You are hot and cold, hard and soft, heart and mind. Whichever road I take, whichever journey I make, whichever path I choose, I will always feel like I can never be with you. Such is the journey the traveller must take to know you can never truly be known until you reach home.

Karma Yoga
CONTRADICTION
Contradiction is when you experience one thing and its opposite in the same moment. You are going forwards and backwards, you are hot and cold, you are lost and found. Only the mind from your mistaken beliefs questions this reality and doubts its validity. Your True Self knows it is possible.

Questions
1.How does it feel to know you cannot ever really grasp God?
2.Do you know you can never be the same as God at this point?
3.Are you aware you are but a tiny spec of dust compared to God?
4.What does it feel like to be small?
5.What does it mean to always know him, yet to never know him?
6.What is a contradiction?
7.How is God a contradiction?
8.Can you be heart and mind?
9.Do you accept that you will always feel like you can never be with God?
10.What does it mean to know?

Today: Know that no matter how much you know, you can never truly know.

·Chapter IV·

Verse 20

Verse
'His form cannot be seen. No one perceives him with the eye. Those who know him through intuition, thus abiding in the heart, become immortal.'

JnaniYoga
Reside within your heart more often now, spend time alone connecting with your heart. Meditate for longer, endure the pain of sitting still, and alone. And, in the stillness of your heart allow God to show himself to you. Let your thoughts rest, your mind slow down. And only be aware of your heart.

Bhakti Yoga
My heart, where my true home is, knows you. I have become so distracted from you I have forgotten where to find you. I go to relentless places that tell me so many untruths, that I then lose myself in all the lies and I lose myself from you. These thoughts that continue on without me round and around they go, and never can I find you when I stop to stand so. My stillness it beguiles me, and leaves me hopeless still, and move I must to find you with all my Divine will.

Karma Yoga
INTUITION
Intuition, the voice of your spiritual heart, knowledge from your True Self pushing up through the illusion of separation and speaking to you. Intuition is to be heard, you can only listen to it, observe it, learn from it. You cannot force it into awareness, it will rise up as if from nowhere.

Questions
1.Why can God's form not be seen?
2.Close your eyes and perceive God, what do you see?
3.What is intuition?
4.How do you abide in the heart?
5.Do you get distracted from your heart?
6.How do you lose yourself in untruths?
7.Are you comfortable with stillness?
8.How is your meditation practice?
9.When you are aware of your heart, what happens?
10.Do you listen to your intuition above your thoughts?

Today: Know your mind will get lost and in the stillness of your heart you can be found.

·Chapter IV·

Verse 21

Verse
**'Some being afraid approach thee, thinking that thou art the unborn.
0 Rudra! Deign to protect me forever with thy benevolent face.'**

JnaniYoga
All the effort and hard work you have put into your realisations should be transforming your perception of your form. When you look at yourself in the mirror there should be a noticeable difference. The perception generated from your old self should have altered considerably, and a new perception should have taken its place. The perception of yourself from your truer Self should be a more complete reflection of your Divine will. Spend time looking in the mirror. Notice how you see yourself. What do you see in your reflection?

Bhakti Yoga
I stand still now and in the waters of your Divine reflection I see myself. My face has become one with yours, my eyes alight with your Divinity, my mouth it speaks of tranquillity. It soothes the torment of all the souls that approach thee for Divine counsel.

Karma Yoga
TRANOUILITY
An ability to experience a soothing, calm energy washing over, and through your whole being. Your Divinity manifests a capacity for stillness. This tranquillity should effortlessly exude out of your being, and be witnessed by others in your presence.

Questions
1.Are people afraid of you?
2.Do people see God in you?
3.Do you feel protected the more you know you are God?
4.Is your face benevolent?
5.Can you feel the waters of your Divine reflection?
6.Do you actually see yourself?
7.How has your face changed?
8.What do you see when you look in your eyes?
9.Are people soothed by your voice?
10.Do you feel tranquil?

Today: Look in the Divine waters of your reflection in the mirror of life and seek Divine counsel.

·Chapter IV·

Verse 22

Verse

'O Audra! Injure not our children, nor our grandchildren, nor our lives, cows and horses, nor slay in thy wrath our valiant men. We invoke thee always with offerings.'

JnaniYoga

Caring for your fellow man may feel like a new concept, or it may be something you feel accustomed to. Whatever your idea of your capacity to care, by now it has grown to an enormous height. And, if you stop and breathe for a minute, and allow yourself to catch your breath, you will notice many things really upset you. As the distractions of your vasanas begin to dissipate, a welling up of compassion rises up from within, and you realise your oneness. Everyone needs you because they are all fighting the same fight, even if they don't know it yet. Reach out and help others in need. Share yourself, as you become aware of everything you care about. Feel God's love pour out of your being as you connect with all of humanities pain.

Bhakti Yoga

This painful war is over, and injuries I must bring, to the everlasting table of your Divine spring. The aches of discontentment leave me now without a trace, the fragments of disillusionment and their scars that I now must face. I leave this war a hero, but rest a while I must for the truth be known to all man this war is not yet over. A battle still to be won, one of enormous size must be faced head on. The battle of despair, hopelessness and fear, that relentlessly continues on for year after year. The battle of our generations, of future kith and kin, that must be waged ahead of time to have a chance to win. I stand alone and fearless in the face of the battles cry, I have a tremendous weapon that in my heart will never die. My weapon is one I forged when time and space stood very still, it is my trusty stead, my friend and it always will, will. My will to be victorious to succeed for you I must, to win this battle for you, oh Brahman, I must trust, I must trust, I must trust.

Karma Yoga
TRUST

When you know you can do it, a relief falls upon you and you believe in yourself. Anything you approach can be overcome, you are capable of great things. 'I know I can,' becomes your mantra for living. Nothing seems impossible .

·Chapter IV·

Questions

1.Do you feel protective towards your fellow man?
2.Do you invoke God with offerings? If so, what are these offerings?
3.Describe the war you have fought?
4.What are your injuries, scars?
5.Are you a hero?
6.Do you want to help future generations with their battle?
7.Do you will yourself to be victorious, to succeed?
8.How much do you want to win?
9.Do you trust?
10.How did you win this battle thus far?

Today: Trust that the battle inside must be won.

·Chapter IV·

Main Point of Chapter IV
THE RELATIONSHIP BETWEEN THE SELF AND VASANAS
The main point being conveyed to you throughout Chapter IV is about your relationship with vasanas from the viewpoint of your SELF. The Self inside all beings must cultivate a deeper, more meaningful relationship with Brahman for Self Realisation to deepen. This relationship is the fourth stage of Self Realisation. This realisation starts with vasanas and an awareness of the need to let them go.

The process now has its goal, and the steps to realise this goal are as follows:

a)Understand your Real Nature.
b)Live according to God's will.
c)See life as magnificent.
d)Push yourself more.
e)Be an individual.
f)Discern between you and God.
g)Experience the unexplainable.
h)Adjust your perceptions.
i)Understand illusion, differentiate the real from the unreal.
j)Explore the concept of Guru.
k)Practice being adequate.
l)Open yourself to love.
m)Observe consciousness.
n)Experience life.
o)Go on an inner adventure.
p)Find motivation to move forward.
q)Desire God.
r)Contemplate your journey.
s)Listen to your heart.
t)See yourself as God.
u)Learn to care about others.

This chapter outlines, and clearly guides you towards an ever greater experience of how to let go of your vasanas, and how to eventually care about the war between good and evil.

·Chapter V·

Verse 1

Verse
'Ignorance verily is mortal. Knowledge verily is immortal. In the imperishable and infinite highest Brahman, knowledge and ignorance are hidden. Entirely different from these is Brahman who contains both ignorance and knowledge.'

JnaniYoga
Take a step back from all that you have become, and notice the mind you reside in, has it changed? Does it light up now when you realise something new? Does it have empty spaces between each thought? Do your thoughts seem more meaningless, or are you more detached from mind experiences? Do you see yourself and your thoughts as separate, apart from each other? Are your thoughts just happening inside your mind without any reason? Can you see the unrealness of the endless chatter that continues throughout your mind?

Bhakti Yoga
Shiva, oh my God Shiva, how have I found myself here, here with you, alone? I am blessed, ever so blessed, be still my beating heart. I am full of your love, your grace resounds throughout my entire being. And Shiva, oh yes Shiva, I am free, I am free, I am free. Free from the shackles, the everyday mundane burdens of Self Realisation. No more, no more, no more do I ever have to toil over the troubles of an absent mind.

·Chapter V·

My mind, oh my mind, what a wonder to behold, an awe inspiring event in your evolution. My mind it is once more free to gaze, to gaze upon your endless streams of Divine Grace, within and without. My consciousness, it exudes the peace and tranquillity of a mind set free, set free, set free. The three Worlds and me, the three worlds and thee.

Karma Yoga
SELF REALISATION
Can you find out who is having the thoughts; who is doing the actions; who is feeling the emotions; who is having the relationships; who is desiring; who is being attached to things, people, places; who is loving; who is fearful? Reaching behind, or through, these transient, impermanent acts and witnessing, observing, an organism that is director of these acts, is driven to do these things, to find out, to experience, to know. This organism of consciousness is the Self and the process above is Realisation. Self Realisation is discovering, through a driven act of searching, who is actually making these things happen. Where are these acts coming from? Where is the origin? On finding the source, the being that is having the thoughts, you realise your True Self. You find out who you are.

Questions
1.What is your mind like today?
2.How has your mind changed?
3.What has changed your mind?
4.Do you experience the unrealness of your mind's endless chatter?
5.Who is having thoughts?
6.Who decides what actions you must take in any given moment?
7.When you go behind your thoughts what do you witness, observe?
8.Are you driven to search for Truth?
9.Have you ever experienced the source of your thoughts, even if only for a moment?
10.Have you ever thought: 'I am God'?

Today: Choose to love your mind.

Verse 2

Verse
'It is he who, being one only presides over every source of production, and every form. He sees the birth of the first born seer of golden colour and endows him with every kind of knowledge at the commencement of the creation.'

·Chapter V·

JnaniYoga

Do you ever allow yourself to be conscious of all that you know? The storehouse of inner knowledge that you have accumulated? Do you feel in awe at everything that you have learnt? With inner knowledge comes an awareness of awe. Awe towards the source of all that wisdom. Its power and glory, the magnitude of such an enormous boon, that God would grant you access to his vast store of Truth. A Truth so powerful, that the mind excites on witnessing this Greatness.Do you ever share your insights, awareness and knowledge with others? Do something, anything, to share what you know.

Bhakti Yoga

It is knowledge. I am full to burst with so much, little did I know of Realisation before. I searched, I ventured, I claimed, I conquered. And yet, what of my goal, I knew nothing of this. The sheer magnitude of my being, it overflows with an abundance of insight, awareness and bliss. My consciousness is an explosion on the page of life, life as I knew it to be no longer a reality. A faded realism of an exalted matter. A matter destined, beyond reason, beyond doubt to dissolve into the Divine streams of your bliss. I cannot believe I am here, I cannot believe here is the experience in my being. I pay homage to your power, to your glory. You have saved me from a cycle of never ending unconsciousness. I am now awake and my duty to serve you for all of my days has fallen upon my soul. My soul has lifted into action, action for you. For you only do I awaken from this deep, deep slumber. I am conscious for you, my dear, dear Lord Shiva, for you and only you.

Karma Yoga

CONSCIOUS

The process of Self Realisation is about making everything unknown, known. Within all beings is a store of knowledge, universal truths, Divine laws or principles. During the path of realising your True Nature it is your job to bring this knowledge out of your unconscious into conscious awareness. Conscious means to be awake, therefore becoming more conscious is waking up this knowledge from its deep, deep slumber. And all of your spiritual practices act like a Divine alarm clock, waking up sleeping realisations. You do not get Realisation, you are Realisation. You just forgot, and now you are remembering.

Questions

1.Do you actually allow yourself to be conscious of your awareness?
2.Do you hide your knowledge from others, or sometimes yourself?
3.Are you afraid of what you know?
4.Are you in awe of the vast bank of knowledge within all beings?
5.Do you realise knowledge lies dormant within, and does not come from outside of you?

·Chapter V·

6.Do you share your knowledge with others?
7.What have you done to share with others?
8.Are you determined to bring up all that is unconscious into a conscious awareness?
9.Are you waking up?
10.How can you wake yourself up more, and wake up others also?

Today: Witness the vast expanse of knowledge within your being, and rejoice at this glory.

Verse 3

Verse
'This God spreads out one net after another in various ways and withdraws it together again in that field. Thus again, having created the rulers, the great soul holds his Lordship overall.'

JnaniYoga
Being awake, feeling alive, singing and dancing through life. Happiness oozing out of your being, the sound of laughter, the smell of success. Celebrate, express your happiness, do something to show yourself how proud you are of yourself, all the hard work. Reward yourself, give yourself a treat, acknowledge your achievement.

Bhakti Yoga
What is this world that I have awoken to? To whom does this world belong? How can it be that it is yours, Oh Shiva, it cannot be so, it cannot be so. The pain, the misery, the suffering. The reality I have found is so, so dearly lost. The mind has become so lonely, so abstract, so conscious of only itself. The self centeredness, the desires, the wants and the needs have so overtaken thee, how can this be? What am I to do in a world such as this? I find myself wondering so much, on how can this be possible with your Grace, so much Grace abundantly spread over so many fields. Fields of awakened consciousness, souls with bound hands and feet, set free to search, to look, to wander, to wonder, to wonder about you and only you. I see now, the point, the point of all this suffering. How can such suffering really exist without you? No more pain, no more misery, no more suffering. Only this can be true without you when you have forgotten yourself. You swim aimlessly without direction, without Grace, through the oceans of forgetfulness and there before you still and conscious, Shiva the fisherman lifts you up into the boat of remembrance and holds you up with arms outstretched towards the heavens of his Supreme universe. And there, in the stars of his Divine home you are awake, awake to your very nature, the latent power of consciousness within, alive in you

·Chapter V·

once more. And then he places you gently, ever so gently, back into the ocean and he lets go. There you find yourself, swimming softly and gently towards life. And life, oh yes your life, it now feels right, no more a struggle, but a joy to behold.

Karma Yoga
JOY
A childlike, carefree whirl of excitement rushing through your entire being. An explosion of blissful consciousness like a firework bursting out of your Self. A genuine, alive high. One that no words can express.

Questions
1.Are you awake?
2.What is happiness?
3.Do you acknowledge your success?
4.Are you proud of your accomplishment?
5.How do you reward yourself?
6.Do you think it is wrong, or egotistical, to give yourself praise?
7.How do you respond to external praise?
8.Are you experiencing joy in your life? 9. Do you ever feel 'high'?
10. How do you share your joy with others?

Today: Know without doubt that when you swim in the waters of life you are never alone.

Verse 4

Verse
'Just as the sun shines, lighting up all quarters above, below and across, so also does that one adorable God, the blessed one, rule over whatever creatures are born from the womb.'

JnaniYoga
Share yourself with others, do your duty. Carry the message of hope and freedom to all that you meet. Do not convert others to your path. This is not the nature of sharing. Share your Self. Be radiant with those you meet. Share your compassion, your wisdom, your insights and awarenesses. Let people know the Divine is real, it exists for all. There are no lost causes, everyone has the capacity for the Divine. Allow people to see your radiance, your light as it shines through your body. Don't hold back, have faith, believe in yourself.

·Chapter V·

Bhakti Yoga
My life is a message of hope and prosperity. One of untold boons and immeasurable pleasures, pleasures not to be gained by mere world endeavours, but immaterial kinds that cannot be qualified. The words I write, the voice I speak, the language I use to communicate is unnecessary to me. The light I radiate out to you now is all that matters. A light so bright that closeness is harmful, a separation is necessary, it is fundamental in realising the True Nature of all born from the womb. A separation so vast and expansive must be sought now, for all to see the creator that can and will bestow Grace on all who seek that awareness and reality for themselves. Now is the time, there is no other time greater than this to reach out with arms outstretched to bask in the glory of our Divine maker.

Karma Yoga
SEPARATION
Distance yourself from God. Observe the vast space between you and him. Look at the lessons still to be learned, notice the terrain yet to be conquered. You need to know that this is your journey, there is much more to do. The road continues, stretches on for miles and miles of unrealised matter. Do not rest, do not think you are there. Separation means to pull away from God, and view the space between you both, registering within your being the route you must take to draw him closer still.

Questions
1.Do you share yourself?
2.What is your duty?
3.What is your message of hope?
4.Do you try to convert people to your path?
5.Do you enjoy being vulnerable?
6.How can you let people know the Divine is real?
7.Do you think you have finished, that your journey is over?
8.Do you get complacent?
9.Looking at the space between you and God, how do you feel?
10.What route are you going to have to take to draw closer to God?

Today: Cultivate separation between you and your chosen God.

Verse 5

Verse
'He, who is the one source of the world, brings to maturity the nature of all and leads creatures who can be brought to maturity to perfection and

·Chapter V·

endows each being with its distinguishing quality and rules this universe.'

JnaniYoga
Acknowledge, be honest with yourself and God, that you have a place inside yourself that resists him. A place where you believe yourself to be God already. Everyone on a spiritual journey at some point thinks themselves Realised, they become arrogant and conceited. Some people even think that they are above God, or do not need him anymore. These behaviours and attitudes come from an ego state, they are natural and are meant to help you to see that you are stuck. Somewhere along your path you experienced something that you couldn't work through, and instead of pushing yourself harder through the obstacle, you created denial. A mechanism of self protection. If you are ready to free yourself from your denial you must fall on your knees and pray to God for the humility to be shown by God exactly what you need to do. This humility will re-engage you with your path, and remind you that you are not yet Realised and still have much work to do.

Bhakti Yoga
Our Individual Self must now realise its One True Nature and make the journey all must eventually take home to their Divine Creator. This is now the time, there has been no better time until now, and there will be no better time than this. You must take up your weapons, you must choose them well, they must reflect all that you know yourself to be. You must summon up all the strength you have available to you, you must release all frustrations, and you must now fight, fight all the inner demons, the darkness in yourself that once prevailed, you must release them to me, hand them over, give them up in surrender to my might, my power and my glory.

Karma Yoga
FIGHT
Expelling a lot of energy on one thing, person, situation. Releasing an enormous amount of energy from yourself onto a situation that is making you feel frustrated. This is what it means to fight. Metaphorically hitting, kicking, pushing and pulling in order to make something shift or get its attention. Fighting inner demons is challenging, and requires a lot of energy. But, resisting them requires much more energy and is very draining and exhausting. Once you have fought your inner demons you find yourself having more energy, and a new feeling of commitment to your path.

Questions
1.Are you honest about your resistance?

·Chapter V·

2.Do you ever think that you are already God, and have no inner demons?
3.Can you be arrogant and conceited?
4.Do you ever think yourself to be above God, or that you do not need him anymore?
5.Are you stuck?
6.Is there an obstacle you could not push through?
7.What is denial, and how do you know if you are in denial?
8.Are you still cultivating humility?
9.Are you fighting hard for God?
10.How are you fighting?

Today: Take responsibility for the fight you must have with the demons that resist Realisation.

Verse 6

Verse
'He is concealed in the Upanishads that are concealed in the Vedas. Hiranyagarbha knows him as the source of himself (or as the source of the Vedas). Those Gods and Seers who realised him in days of yore, became indentified with him and verily became immortal.'

JnaniYoga
Meditate on the verses now. This is an advanced practice that you are now ready to try. As you go through the chapters and study the verses you are gaining confidence and knowledge. But, there is a knowledge that resides even deeper still, that to access this knowledge requires great faith and self belief . So, read a verse from the Upanishad and then close your eyes and meditate for at least half an hour. Allow the verse to speak to you, it will show you its true meaning, its essence as it was intended. But, you have to listen carefully to your intuition and trust what you hear. Once your meditation is complete, write down what you heard, saw, felt. This is the essence of the Upanishads.

Bhakti Yoga
These scriptures I write about are beyond words, beyond explanation. The commentary I am referring to does no justice to the Realisation found in the experience of them. There are no descriptions that can adequately refer to the reality of these verses. The reality of this text is beyond comprehension. No God realised being could ever justify themselves with the ramblings of this page. I look at you, the letters, words, sentences and I am profoundly disappointed.

·Chapter V·

A disappointment that I fear is metaphorical in nature. A reflection of a reality based outside the realms of consciousness, one of ignorance and arrogance. How can anyone truly believe that God would or could be limited to a manmade invention such as words? God has to be, and must be experienced in the hearts of all to truly be known, to truly be conscious, to truly be realised. My heartfelt words say to you read, read, read. But know this, that not one realisation will be given for mere reading. The reading then has to be assimilated somehow, and the how is so much more necessary. Identify your very own Self with each essence known to you that you connect with on reading this text. Go past the words and resonate with what is inside each and every one of them. That essence that cannot be materialised is the Upanishads, that essence is Brahman, that essence is you.

Karma Yoga
WORDS
Words are forms, just like the physical form of the body. Inside each word, each letter, is its True Nature, its intention, who it really is. The consciousness of a word communicates to you, the reader. The Upanishad verses are compiled using the words of God. Inside the verse you will experience God.

Questions
1.Have you tried meditating on the verses, rather than just reading the words?
2.How do you feel about advancing your practice?
3.Do you feel more confident, more knowledgeable?
4.Do you believe in yourself more, and have more faith in God?
5.Do you trust your intuition?
6.What is the essence of the Upanishads?
7.Do you understand that words are also form?
8.Can you see that within all form resides God?
9.How do you experience God through form?
10.Is the formless inside everything?

Today: Go past the words that you read in this verse, and resonate with the essence of what is written.

Verse 7

Verse
'He (the individual soul), who is attached with the qualities, performs actions for the sake of fruits and enjoys the fruits of his own actions. Though he is really the Lord of life, he becomes bound by the three gunas, assumes various forms and wanders about through the three paths on account of his own actions.'

·Chapter V·

JnaniYoga
You are almost home now, the space between you and God has reduced. The light at the end of the road is more visible to you, you can clearly see your destination. So, now what do you do? Well, now you have to make an everlasting, definite commitment to your path. Which yoga are you going to practice, that will ensure your safe arrival back with God? There are so many variations, so many choices, that you must sit down and study your options. Draw from your existing experiences, accept what you know about yourself already, research all the yogas, and learn about those who are practicing them. And, finally, after you have exhausted all your options, speak with God and ask him to help you. If you have a Guru, ask them to discuss it with you.

Bhakti Yoga
There are three worlds given freely to us, and three paths upon which these worlds rest. The primary and most austere world, is the cosmic in nature, and therefore the purity of its Divinity more refined. This world rests on a narrow, astutely defined path, one of knowledge and immense wisdom. The second world and the most fruitful, available and rich with spiritual boons aplenty, is the individual souls territory, the path it rests on is one love and absolute heartfelt devotion to the Lord of All. And, finally, and not least important is the third world, a world full of obstacles, potholes and hidden agendas. The path this world has chosen to rest on is one of action, and selfless service to the Divine. A truly Realised Being would tell you with all certainty that to tread the paths of all, and ultimately to conquer all three worlds one must walk along all paths. Your mind must walk along the first path, your heart the second, and last but not least, your body the third. It is true also, as is always the way in spiritual terms, that nothing is quite as linear or logical as one might hope for. A sadhaka may follow one path, they may immerse their entire being to that path, and dedicate their whole life towards it, but, one must be careful not to lose sight of the goal, not to forget what they are here to do. As to only experience one of these worlds is hard, and to succeed one must be extremely focused. And, in times such as these, where distractions are around every corner, caution should be applied when choosing, because this is the most important choice you will ever make.

Karma Yoga
PATH
A path is a stable, level ground that enables you to walk through rocky terrain. It takes you from one place (where you are), to another (where you want to be). A path makes the journey from A to B much easier, and also clearly defines the way. A path is essential.

·Chapter V·

Questions
1.How does it feel to be almost home?
2.Can you see the light at the end of the road?
3.Are you afraid to commit to a path?
4.Do you doubt your ability to choose?
5.Do you trust that God will show you the way?
6.How do you feel about researching yogas?
7.What do you know about yourself that can help you to choose?
8.Do you resonate with anyone you have heard about, such as a famous person, a friend, a teacher etc?
9.How do you feel about the ground being more stable on your path?
10.What is your path?

Today: Choose your path home carefully, evaluate every option and apply your innate powers of discernment wisely.

Verse 8

Verse
'Subtle as the point of an awl, brilliant like the sun, he alone is perceived even as another (different from the universal soul) of the size of a thumb, endowed with egoism and sankalpa, on account of the limitation of the intellect and heart.'

JnaniYoga
Repetition is a prerequisite to the path of yoga. Bhakti yoga is the practice of expressing love towards God. Karma yoga is the practice of offering all actions to God. Jnani yoga is the practice of discrimination between the real and the unreal. (My personal teachings do not support the practice of pure Raja yoga in the Western world. Raja yoga is the practice of focusing solely on the breath, and your inner life. I feel that people in the West need to engage with the outside world, and becoming immersed in days of meditation would isolate you from the society of the West, which desperately needs your help). Just like the practice of Ashtanga yoga, or any other form of yoga designed to create a more adequate physical form, one needs to practice daily, repeating over and over again to reap the benefits. Even though the benefits are not as visible as with the practice of physical yoga, in time you will find, or may already have found, the benefits are very visible - your emotions change, your world changes and your thinking changes respectively.

Bhakti Yoga
There are no other words but this, there are no other thoughts but this, there are no other feelings but this, not this, not that.

·Chapter V·

Karma Yoga
MANTRA

If you can imagine that your mind is like a muscle, and that thoughts are fatty pockets that have built up around the muscle due to laziness, eating the wrong kinds of food metaphorically, and a lack of yogic practice. Then, mantras are the weights that transform the thoughts back into muscle. Through hard work, sweat and a little pain, a mantra can destroy thoughts very easily. Mantras chip away at thoughts, the energy within the words of the mantra acts like a dissolvent to the energy within the thoughts.

Questions

1.Are you repetitive with your yoga? Are you religious with your practice?
2.Describe your thoughts, feelings, attitudes towards your yoga.
3.How does your yoga engage you with the outside world?
4.What is your daily spiritual practice?
5.What benefits do you see during, or after, your practice?
6.Do you practice any mantras?
7.Do you value the ancient mantras that have been used for thousands of years?
8.What is your thinking like?
9.What do you do to have a cleaner, purer mind?
10.How are you limiting your spiritual practice?

Today: Repeat the words 'Neti, neti' as a mantra.

Verse 9

Verse
'That individual soul is as subtle as the hundredth part of the point of a hair divided a hundred times. Yet he is (in essence) infinite. He has to be known.'

JnaniYoga

It is so easy to fall into the trap of comparing your journey to that of others. How can anything so unique as your own individual path possibly compare to that of anyone else? No one else has your karma, all karma is absolutely individual and unique. Just like the human fingerprint, it is possible that of all the billions in the world's population, not one path is exactly the same. In God's infinite wisdom, and power, he has designed a path just for you, so that you can know him personally, and build an individual relationship with him. Don't get caught up in the ever so common trap of competing with those travelling with you on a spiritual path. Practice supporting others, and not comparing or measuring yourself against them.

·Chapter V·

But compare yourself to where you have been yourself and where you need to go.

Bhakti Yoga
To know you is to know yourself, time must not be wasted on mere analysis of all that surrounds you. There is so much to be sought within your very own Self, so much time is wasted on looking outside, and seeking awareness of all that you are, and all that you can be. All that you can be is only available when you look to yourself, please do not waste another moment of despair and anguish on futile observations of anyone, anything or anywhere, but yourself. You hold all the cards. The cards of realisations are to bet upon only in your name and in your honour, do not gamble your money on judgements, misconceptions, mistaken ideas of what is real for anyone other than you. Leave the rest to me, I will take care of all your surroundings. Put your trust in me, I will make sure your home is safe and warm for you to rest. Place your bets on me, I will be sure to be the surest winner for all eternity.

Karma Yoga
JOURNEY
When you decide to go somewhere you must find out the address, refer to a map of the area, prepare the necessary equipment, choose your transport and make travel plans. The same is required for your spiritual travel. This is the journey. The address is God's home; the map of the area is your insight and knowledge of what God is, and where he resides; the necessary equipment is your spiritual tools; your choice of transport is your yoga; and your travel plans are your attitudes towards your journey. Plan your journey well, cover every eventuality, and enjoy your travel.

Questions
1.Do you compare yourself with others?
2.How do you relate to your individual karma?
3.Can you believe God is powerful and designs every path according to your individual need?
4.How do you support your fellow travellers?
5.What is God's address?
6.Have you located a map of the area, what is it?
7.What necessary equipment do you need for your journey?
8.Have you chosen your transport?
9.What are your travel plans?
10.Are you looking forward to your travels?

Today: Do not waste precious time looking outside, take your journey within your very own Self.

·Chapter V·

Verse 10

Verse
'He is neither female nor male, nor neuter. Whatever body he takes, with that he becomes identified or joined or connected.'

JnaniYoga
Instead of spending moments in relationships comparing yourself to their formed self, spend time looking beyond the form, see beyond all form that the Atman is in all things . When you meet people consciously look for their Atman, practice seeing their Divinity. Compare your Divinity to theirs, and recognise that it is one. The Divine that you see is in you, elevate your relationships to this place of Truth, and they will improve. Your perception of yourself will also improve .

Bhakti Yoga
Do not imagine that form , relationships, gender or ideas can ever constitute a reality such as the Self. The Self cannot be confined to matter, only the beyond of matter can ever be that One True Reality you have been searching for. There is no other truth than this, there is no other truth than this, there is no other truth than this.

Karma Yoga
BEYOND
There are many perceived obstacles on your path, and in life. Looking past these obstacles, taking your awareness behind them is what is real, it is what is beyond .

Questions
1.Do you only see the form?
2.Do you spend time looking beyond the form?
3.Can you see the Atman in all things?
4.Can you see the Atman in people?
5.What is the Divinity you see?
6.Can you recognise the oneness of Divinity?
7.How does your perception of yourself alter when you see the Divinity in others?
8.Do you get stuck with perceived obstacles?
9.Do you look behind obstacles?
10.Do you notice what is real?

Today: In your search for Self realise Self is beyond all form, and yet is within all form.

·Chapter V·

Verse 11

Verse
'By means of thoughts, contact sight and delusion, the embodied soul assumes successively, various forms in various places, in accordance with his actions, just as the body grows by the use of food and drink.'

JnaniYoga
If you want to succeed, do not waste time with transitory desires. Be serious about your practice. Organise your days, weeks, months and prioritise your spiritual practice. Place it first, above all else. See the difference it makes.

Bhakti Yoga
All the while you seek these transitory nuances the time is accumulating, you are feeding a habit of untold destruction, every moment given to thought adds so many years on your journey of an embodied soul. Your thoughts, your relationships, your senses, your mind all accumulate unwanted time, time you do not want or need.

Karma Yoga
TIME
Time is precious, time is energy gifted to us by God. We must use this energy well, and take advantage of how much we have been given. Every day is a blessing. Live every day as if it were the only day you have.

Questions
1.Do you still feel passionately about succeeding?
2.Are you beginning to waste time?
3.Are you giving in to desires more?
4.Are you maintaining a serious spiritual practice?
5.Are you serious about your spiritual practice?
6.Organise your days, how does it feel?
7.Is your spiritual practice a priority?
8.Do you value time?
9.Do you honour time as a gift from God?
10.Give thanks for your gift of time.

Today: Do not waste precious time cultivating unnecessary distractions from your path.

·Chapter V·

Verse 12

Verse
'The individual soul chooses or assumes many forms, gross and subtle, according to his own qualities, the qualities of his actions and the qualities of his mind. The cause of union with these forms is found to be still another.'

JnaniYoga
There is a Divine plan for everyone. A predetermined set of directions, an intuitive guide rests within your heart, guiding you through this plan. This plan is not conscious, it is not something that can be written down and studied. Most of your guidance will be sporadic, and moment to moment. Accept the plans you make may have to change, don't be rigid with your own guidance. Allow for the Divine to enter at any moment, and for all your plans to change.

Bhakti Yoga
Why place value on anything that will fade away, wither and die. Is not the value you misplace to be directed inwards to a place where there is no other, where only you are to be found? Are you not enough, are you not enough, and are you enough, if God made you in his own image, as a reflection of him? If there is a spark of God within you, and you cannot see it or will it into your awareness, is it not your divine duty to realise it into awareness, is it not your destiny to move every mountain until you have uncovered the truth of your intended self, the reality of your pure essence experienced into existence, for is it not the reality intended for you that is worthy of experience? Are you not led, drawn, pulled, to a place of realness within your very own self where God can be realised? Who are you not to manifest the intention of God, who are you to deny God his plans for you, who are you to realise nothing of what and whom you really are? Are you not tired now, do you not want to rest your mind upon the threshold of Gods divine home and concentrate all of your senses on his supreme heartfelt desire for you to come home now to him? 'I love you', he says, 'I want you back in my arms, I want to hold you and protect you from all the realities you thought were me, and find you once more in my Divine plan.'

Karma Yoga
PLANS
Your logic organises future events according to its will.

Questions
1.Do you accept there is a Divine plan?
2.Are you aware of your intuition guiding you?

·Chapter V·

3.Where does the guidance come from for your intuition?
4.Does this Divine plan ever become conscious, even for a moment?
5.Do you accept that the plans you personally make may need to change?
6Are you rigid with plans?
7.Are you open to Divinity guiding you?
8.Do you logically organise future events?
9.Are you wilful when it comes to planning?
10.Are you ready to live God's plan for you?

Today: Realise nothing, realise everything, realise something of who you really are, who God created you to be.

Verse 13

Verse
'He who knows him, who has no beginning and no end, who creates the world in the midst of chaos, who assumes many forms and who alone envelops the universe is freed from all fetters.'

JnaniYoga
Are you ready to reflect on the idea now that you are already Realised? And, that in every moment you are Realised? A veil of ignorance has fallen upon you, and you have forgotten that you know. Spend time in reflection, ask yourself: 'Am I Realised?'

Bhakti Yoga
I do not lie to you, I have always told you the truth, and I will never let you down. My place I have saved for you, my place of sanctuary has always been, and always will be here within us both. The place where we are one. It is the place where it all began, and it will be the place where it all ends. There will be no more beginnings for our self, no more endings. All will become seamless, effortless, and restful, we will abide as one being with no end in sight. Everlasting, everlasting, everlasting.

Karma Yoga
ABIDE
Where do you live? Where do you call home? Wherever you call home is where you live and abide.

Questions
1.What is sanctuary?

·Chapter V·

2.Do you have somewhere special where you feel safe?
3.Are you restful within yourself?
4.What does it mean: 'You are already Realised'?
5.How can every moment be a Realised moment?
6.What is this veil of ignorance?
7.How did you forget all that you know?
8.Are you Realised?
9.Where is home to you?
10.Are you home?

Today: See inside the moment where the end, the middle and the beginning no longer exist for you.

Verse 14

Verse
'Those who know the God who is to be realised by direct intuitive perception, who is incorporeal or immaterial, who is the cause of existence and non-existence, who is all-blessed and the cause of the origin of the (sixteen) parts, are freed from further embodiment.'

JnaniYoga
Let go of shame, and all things that tell you that you are small and inadequate, even just for a moment, be big! Allow the enormity of your being to burst out of your body and imagine it raises up above your head and into the sky. Feel the enormous power that you are able to generate, a consciousness of Truth beyond your form, and realise this is a vision of you.

Bhakti Yoga
I am to be found now, and only now. There is no other now, there is no better now, the only now is here. I am in the moment, where all of time stands still, all of space contracts into an unfathomable entity of consciousness, where all of you becomes all of me, where you and me become one. Where can we become, the becoming is upon us, our very existence has ceased, our realities have merged, our consciousness has reached the heights of the gods. The everliving reaches inside of our being and rips out all false notions of separation, a oneness of great magnitude envelops our consciousness and nothing, but nothing, can stand before us.

Karma Yoga
GOD
God is a word, a concept that defines Truth. Everything that is factual is God.

·Chapter V·

Everything that educates us is God. God is a term, it defines us.

Questions

1.Do you experience shame?
2.Can you feel small, or inadequate, within yourself?
3.Have you ever experienced yourself as big?
4.Can you visualise your soul bursting out of your body?
5.What is the vision you have of yourself?
6.What is God?
7.How are you God?
8.Do you believe God exists?
9.What happens when you say the word God?
10.Can you live openly with God in your life?

Today: Know with all certainty that you are God.

·Chapter V·

Main Point of Chapter V

THE RELATIONSHIP WITH REALISATIONS FROM THE VIEWPOINT OF YOUR SELF

The main point conveyed to you throughout Chapter V is about your relationship with Realisations from the viewpoint of your SELF. The SELF inside all beings must cultivate a deeper, more meaningful relationship with Brahman for Self Realisation to deepen. This relationship is the fifth stage of Self Realisation. This realisation starts with Self Realisation , and an awareness of the unrealness of all thoughts.

The process now has its goal, and the steps to realise this goal are as follows:

a)Become conscious of your awareness.
b)Experience great joy.
c)Learn to distance yourself from God.
d)Fight your inner demons .
e)Meditate on the verses.
f)Commit to your chosen path.
g)Repetitive practice of yoga.
h)Plan your journey.
i)Look beyond form.
j)Appreciate time.
k)Accept your Divine plan.
l)Abide in God's home.
m) Define what is God.

This chapter outlines, and clearly guides you towards an ever greater experience of realising the unrealness of your thoughts, and the realness of God.

·Chapter VI·

Verse 1

Verse
'Some deluded thinkers speak of Nature, and others speak of time as the cause of the universe; but it is the glory of God by which this Brahma - wheel revolves.'

JnaniYoga
Being in the world, but not of the world, is the goal of Self Realisation. There is a world outside of your spiritual practice, it does exist. It exists as God intended it to be. But, it does exist alone. There is also a Divine world, that rests detached and observing this material world. It looks on, and patiently helps, supports and guides those still searching through the material world, who are looking for the Divine. You must live within this material world, but have a firm hand holding onto the Divine world. This is necessary to maintain your insights, awarenesses and knowledge thus far. If your hand slips for a moment, all can be lost in the illusion that the Divine world does not really exist.

Bhakti Yoga
Oh my God Brahman, I cannot speak to you of such atrocities as the ones I have just witnessed, the might of the ego world is powerful beyond measure. It has sunken into my being, and took a hold of the very core of me. I am completely taken over, I am lost. The vastness, the enormity, the sheer force of such a thing has stripped me of my life force. I am fighting inside, I can hear the battle cries roar

·Chapter VI·

aloud as my being resists all that it stands for and more. A loss am I, a loss am I, a loss am I. I cannot comprehend the power that I must reckon myself with. I am completely disgusted at what it has become. The energy misused, increasing its weight and velocity, I am saddened and pained for you, my loving teacher, friend and companion. I must muster up all my power, I must fight the demons of anger and rage, I must delve into the darkness and wrench out all the light I can find. And , I can, I can find the light, the light inside that is you and I can reach that light inside and I can yearn, yearn for more and the light will grow, it must grow evermore for you, oh Brahman. I must know only you. I must begin with the smallest of lights, and then I must will upon all else to expand my tiny atom of light upwards, towards you and you will fill me with the light of yourself, that is beyond this seemingly powerful darkness, and I will be with you once more, I will be with you again!

Karma Yoga
BRAHMAN

Brahman is the creator, the sustainer and the destroyer of all three worlds. He is all the aspects of the Divine. He is the almighty God with whom all things rest. He is unobtainable, you cannot reach him, feel him, think of him, or touch him. The only way to know him is through a knower of Brahman, a preceptor. A guide who has met him, and knows him and can introduce you to him. But, only if you are a clear vessel.

Questions

1.What is your relationship with the world?
2.Are you attached to the world?
3.During your spiritual practice are you aware of the material world?
4.Do you maintain a healthy distance from the material world?
5.Are you holding onto your awareness of the Divine world?
6.Do you fear losing all that you have come to know?
7.What is your perception of Brahman?
8.How do you feel that Brahman is unobtainable, unless through a knower of Brahman?
9.Do you know a knower of Brahman?
10.How much do you depend on your knower of Brahman (preceptor)?

Today: Know that however much it appears to be more powerful than you, the darkness can never ever grow further than the Divine light of that one true reality called God, Brahman.

·Chapter VI·

Verse 2

Verse
'It is at the command of him, who always envelops this world, who is all knowing, the Lord of time, possessor of qualities, omniscient, that this work (creation) unfolds itself which is called or thought as earth, water, fire, air and ether.'

JnaniYoga
Submerging yourself in the energy of love and devotion will help keep you afloat at all times. Dwelling in this energy keeps you away from harm, and prevents your mind becoming lost and confused. The only guarantee to success is cultivating an awareness of this energy, and the power within you that rises up, because it is this power that enables you to do things that you did not feel were possible before. It lets you see yourself as you really are, giving you glimpses of your real Self keeps you going. It motivates you to remain steadfast on your path.

Bhakti Yoga
It is so painful to be in this body without so many moments filled with sensory activity. My body it feels as though it will burst open at any time. My heart that once pounded with life force energy no longer grips my soul. I cannot feel you, I cannot hear you, I cannot smell, touch or see you anywhere, anymore. I need you Brahman, my arms are outstretched in eager anticipation for your return to me, your return to thee. I wait on the porch of my body like a child eagerly awaiting the return of a loving expected parent. And as I wait, and wait, and wait it begins once more. The rounds of recycled waste have passed The recycling of my sensory experiences are transformed into a glance, a gaze, a moment of truth when I awake to all that you are, and I know once more with all certainty that you never left me alone. I was always with you, but my mind had ventured out to a lost world, one of distractions and mistaken beliefs. I am home with you now, no longer on the porch of my body, but calmly, peacefully sitting with you at the hearth of your womb, where I am full of your love. Your love has performed a miracle on my soul and again I can feel my heart pounding, the beats, the rhythm is familiar and expected. I am in love with you, I am happy, the bliss I am is you, oh Brahman, yes it is you.

Karma Yoga
DEVOTION
Devotion is like a safety net. Developing devotion towards a knower of Brahman keeps you out of harm's way, it protects you from your lower nature, and the ignorance still inside that can lie to you and lead you back towards darkness.

·Chapter VI·

Once devotion has grown, you receive the energy of the object of your devotion inside yourself. And, it feels as if it were your own. You are allowed to use this energy for your journey home.

Questions

1.What is the energy of love and devotion?
2.Do you submerge yourself in this energy?
3.Can you see that you are kept from harm's way?
4.Do you fear your mind becoming lost and confused?
5.Describe your awareness of this energy.
6.Do you feel powerful?
7.What are you now capable of doing that you did not know possible?
8.Are you motivated and steadfast on your path?
9.Are you devoted to a knower of Brahman?
10.Through devotion you receive your preceptor's energy, what does this feel like?

Today: Remember that this world that has become so real is part of a larger atmosphere that you may not always know, an atmosphere of love and devotion.

Verse 3

Verse

'He creates this work and rests again, having entered into union with principle after principle, with one, with two, with three, or with eight, with time too and with the subtle qualities of the mind.'

JnaniYoga

Being in the energy of love and devotion is one of the most beautiful experiences possible in this human form. But, what happens when you fall, and you forget once more that you are loved? What happens when you are full of despair, and your mind is full of activity, and you cannot remember how to get back to that loved place? When these times come and they inevitably will, you have to surrender once more to the power. You have to remember that you were only borrowing it, and that you did something to lose it. It was never really yours, it was only on loan, until you found it on your own.

Bhakti Yoga

My mind it rages forth towards so many painful images, ideas, concepts, beliefs, thoughts. I am suffering Brahman, I feel so abandoned, so lost. My mind, my head, it hurts, please I beg of you, have mercy on my afflictions. I have sinned, my mind is tainted, it is not fit for you to enter. I lust, I desire, I think so many bad things. I am not worthy of your love. I do not want these sufferings anymore. I beg of you, I prostrate before you, I promise I will repent, I will move every mountain of pain with the strength of your love coursing through my mind. I must have you, and you alone. I must need you, and you alone. I am attached to things I no longer want. I am powerless. I will them to leave but still they resist my chants, my mantras, my surrender. I cannot understand why they resist you. Why do they persist, why do I have an unwelcome guest in my mind. Why can I not simply request them to leave? I say to you now, leave and never come back. With doubt and fear surrounding me my faith has waned, I cannot assert myself upon their relentlessness. I beg once more, and again and again. Leave me alone, walk a different path, follow a different route, take yourself and GO. I must be frank with you now, I am firm, I am steadfast. Leave now and never return, you served me well when I did not realise that your service would cause me so much misery. Now I realise, I realise, I realise. I do not need you and I will never need you again.

Karma Yoga
PROSTRATE
Prostrate means to crawl back on hands and knees along the floor towards your preceptor, and ultimately towards God. So many people become complacent, especially if they are close to a preceptor. They begin to feel as if the preceptor's energy is their own. And forget it is a gift on loan to them, to treasure and keep safe. Prostrating is an act given to one's preceptor to remind oneself that the power is theirs, and theirs alone. They worked hard and through their hard work met and merged with Brahman. To be like them you must also work hard, and not rely on their rewards, but create your own.

Questions
1.Describe what it is like being in the energy of love and devotion.
2.Do you remember the last time you fell back into ignorance? What was it like?
3.Describe despair when ignorant.
4.Do you surrender easily?
5.Are you aware you are only loaning your preceptors energy?
6.Have you ever prostrated?
7.Do you become complacent?
8.What is complacency like?
9.Do you acknowledge your preceptors hard work?
10.Do you prostrate at the lotus feet of your preceptor?

Today: Firmly assert that you do not need anything other than God, and when you doubt, or fear, be steadfast and never give in again.

·Chapter VI·

Verse 4

Verse
'He gives the start to creation associated with the three Gunas and orders all things. He causes destruction of the work in the absence of the Gunas and remains apart in his essence after destruction.'

JnaniYoga
Whether your preceptor be dead or alive; a leader of an organised religion; a Guru; an Avatar; a God or Goddess; nature; Jesus; Allah; Buddha; Shiva etc, you must share the message that they teach, or have taught. If you are a Catholic, share the Bible. If you are a Hindu, share the Vedas. If you are a devotee of Sri Aurobindo, share his teachings. (The list of possible preceptors is long, and one cannot possibly list all here. But, all are equal and of value). Whatever your choice of preceptor, you cannot possibly deepen your level of devotion without sharing their message in whatever they guide you to do. Find a way to share your preceptor's message. Research, explore, and then do it.

Bhakti Yoga
Everything, absolutely everything happens and is happening for a Divine reason. There are no effects without the will of Brahman. Every moment is a creation from Brahman, to Brahman, for Brahman. All the ramblings of a tiny mind are nothing, absolutely nothing in comparison to the will of Brahman. I cannot believe I lost my way, I mistook a mindless mind as you Brahman. The mind it has learnt so many tricks, so many ways and means to manipulate the sadhaka. It's like an organism that was created for good, and in that experience of goodness it had to, just had to know itself even more, so it created the opposite, badness. And, badness grew and grew so vast, and so wild, that the original organism lost itself within the darkness. And it forgot your original intention for itself to be the light, to be the good. I must help you, oh Brahman, my friend, my love, to remind those mistaken, who have mistook the darkness for the truth. I must remind them the truth is within the darkness, you are there, a constant light, so bright that just one glance is enough to remember. I remember you, oh Brahman, I remember your love for me, for all mankind. I remember your Grace, your wisdom, your tenderness. I am totally in love with you, oh Brahman, and only you. I want you to merge with me and to remove the veil of ignorance from my eyes, so I can see in all your glory who you really are.

Karma Yoga
IGNORANCE
Ignorance, what is ignorance? Is it not when the Truth is hidden, when the truth

eludes you? Even though the truth is there, you cannot see it. Do not allow yourself to become ignorant again. You have worked too hard to give into laziness. Study your preceptors teaching daily, immerse yourself in it. But, remember the best way to stay in remembrance of it is to share it.

Questions

1.What is a preceptor?
2.Who, or what, have you chosen as your preceptor?
3.What is their message?
4.Are you sharing their message with others?
5.Do you value your preceptor?
6.Have you extensively researched your preceptor and their teachings?
7.What way do they ask you to share their teachings?
8.How are you ignorant?
9.Are you lazy?
10.What are your preceptor's teachings?

Today: I must remind you that the darkness that you have fallen within is in essence the truth, and that you can return to the light once you realise this is so.

Verse 5

Verse

'He is the beginning, the origin of the causes by which (the body) is united (with the soul). He is beyond the three divisions of time (past, present, future). He is without parts also. The adorable lord, who appears as the wand, who is the source of all creatures and abides in his own heart, is perceived by him who meditates and worships in his heart previously.'

JnaniYoga

Looking up is a good place to be. It keeps your ego in check, humility stronger, and arrogance has nowhere to go. By now God is real for you, and your belief is growing. You know that having a power greater than yourself in life is of much more benefit to you, than not having known this power. Nurture a sense of awe, keep looking up in wonderment.

Bhakti Yoga

I must worship you now my beloved. I must lay down my ignorance and surrender to your holiness. I must sing out in praise of your name Brahman, Brahman, Brahman. I adore you and all that you are, my being is in complete awe and wonderment at your beauty.

·Chapter VI·

You radiate such light towards me and all the darkness vanishes. I want for nothing, no one, but you. May all my life be in worship of you, may all my being lay down in self abandon at your lotus feet.

Karma Yoga
PRAISE
Thank you, thank you. You are so amazing, wonderful. I could not live without you. I am so grateful that you exist. This is praise. How often do you praise God?

Questions
1.Do you look up at God?
2.How does your ego react?
3.Is your humility stronger?
4Are you working on eliminating arrogance?
5.Is God real for you?
6.Are you in awe and wonderment at the power that is God?
7.Do you thank God?
8.How do you express your gratitude towards God?
9.How do you praise God?
10.List what you are grateful for.

Today: Surrender to Brahman and worship his holiness.

Verse 6

Verse
'Highest and other than the world - tree, time and forms is he from whom this universe proceeds, the source of all virtues, the destroyer of all sins, the Lord of all good qualities - know him as in one's self, as the immortal abode of all the universe.'

JnaniYoga
Only the ego would hold onto control. Only the ego would resist reverence towards God. It was made solely for this purpose, but to succeed at realising your True Nature the ego must be destroyed. The ego was only meant to keep you safe in an unreal world, once that world is realised the ego cannot exist. Giving oneself to God requires a relinquishment of the ego.

Bhakti Yoga
And as I abandon myself, and give myself totally to you in worship, with absolute reverence and respect, I realise the Self in me. And, in the realisation I am one with

your Grace. I cannot but praise, and give thanks for your greatness, your power and your glory. That you would come down into my world and give of yourself so abundantly to free me from my blindness, to release me from my prison, to know me as oneself.

Karma Yoga
RESPECT
To know I could not succeed without you, and how I treat you. My treatment towards you, and how that treatment reflects my absolute need for you. This is respect. Do you respect God? Do you respect your preceptor? How do you treat them?

Questions
1.Is your ego controlling?
2.Does your ego resist being reverent towards God?
3.Why do you have an ego?
4.How do you feel about destroying your ego?
5.Has your ego kept you safe?
6.How much have you realised the realness of the world?
7.Can you relinquish your ego to God?
8.Can you succeed without God?
9.How do you treat God?
10.Do you respect God? If so, how do you show it?

Today: I give thanks and praise. I offer my reverence and respect as small tokens to your greatness.

Verse 7

Verse
'May we know him, the transcendent and adorable master of the world, who is the great supreme Lord of all Lords, the supreme deity of all deities and the supreme ruler of all rulers.'

JnaniYoga
The ego wilfully tries to maintain a sense of I, a separateness from all of God's creation. This must not be mistaken with the sense of I (the Atman) that manifests as a result of knowing God. There are so many obvious distinctions between these two 'I's. The egoic 'I' serves only its selfish, self centred needs, it is all about me and mine. The Atman's 'I' serves the Self in all, it seeks to know itself and its Divine Nature. It cares about others and realises that others care about it.

·Chapter VI·

Bhakti Yoga

As I worship you, I realise you, and the more I worship you, the more I am in awe of you. How magnificent you are that you can transform a mind full of suffering so effortlessly into a mind full of love. The bliss I experience whilst I am with you. I cannot bear to be without you. Imagining a world without you now seems so painful. I must focus, focus all of my consciousness upon you, only when all of my being is centred on you can I ever truly know you, can I ever truly say 'I am with you.' And be with you, I must, I must be with you always and forever. You are the supreme ruler of all rulers, there is nothing that compares to you and nothing that ever will.

Karma Yoga
BOW DOWN

Gently, reconnecting, plugging your Self back into the source of creation, is to bow down. This procedure of elegantly bowing down relinquishes control of the egoic 'I', and the very act itself seeks to serve only God. Being a servant of God is like no other service. One is transformed instantly into the Atman .

Questions

1.Do you maintain an egoic sense of 'I'?
2.Do you feel separate from God's creation?
3.Do you sense your Atman's sense of 'I'?
4.How do you differentiate between the two?
5.Describe the egoic 'I'.
6.Describe the Atman's 'I' .
7.Do you care about others?
8.Are you gentle with God?
9.How do you connect with God?
10.Do you enjoy being God's servant?

Today: Accept it is ok to revere something, to bow down and surrender to something as almighty as Brahman.

Verse 8

Verse

'No action (effect) or organ (karanam) of his is found. There is not seen his equal nor a superior. His great power is declared (in the Vedas) to be of various kinds. His knowledge, strength and action are described as inherent in him.'

·Chapter VI·

JnaniYoga
Experience of Brahman is very addictive. The experience of Brahman through one's preceptor is very addictive. There is nothing like it. There before you an almighty surge of absolute love, your presence alone transmitting such love as a direct result of experience. A will so abundantly submerges, a will to immerse others in this light. A need so great to see light in all that you meet. No longer settling for so much darkness, a desire for light everywhere takes hold and grips you, and even starts to control your own selfish needs. Overwhelmed, your needs become irrelevant, and God's needs become a priority.

Bhakti Yoga
It is so hard to describe you, to define you. I am frustrated, and at a loss. I desperately want to show you to the world of ignorant souls. I so crave the need to share you with as many tiny lights. I need them to know the beauty that lies deep down inside, the beauty of their maker that I find impossible to deny. I have found the everything in heart, mind and deed, all of my becoming has been a mighty seed. I want to sing aloud a chorus of worship and praise, so that we can rejoice together for the rest of our days. Please Brahman, the saviour supreme, show me how to do God's will, I must attempt as all else has failed, as there are so many tired hearts to fill. And fill, and fill I must with the nectar of your Grace, to witness the transformation on not just my own face.

Karma Yoga
SHARE
How are you sharing your preceptor's message now it is time to share directly? Sharing means not to keep something to one's self. It means to give it away to others. To keep this energy of love and devotion, you must share it. If you do not share it, you are telling God that there isn't enough, you are believing in lack. And, if you believe in lack for long enough, you will start to experience lack in yourself, in your life, and in your relationship with God. Find a way to share directly with others what has helped you to reach this inner state that has become so normal for you.

Questions
1.What is your experience of Brahman?
2.Are you addicted to Brahman and/or your preceptor?
3.How does your preceptor transmit love?
4.Are you addicted to light?
5.Do you want to see light in others?
6.Are you settling for too much darkness?
7.Are God's needs a priority?

·Chapter VI·

8.Do you believe in lack?
9.How are you sharing your preceptors teaching's directly?
10.Explain how your preceptor's teachings have helped you.

Today: Share the almighty Brahman with as many souls as you can.

Verse 9

Verse
'There is no master of his in this world, no ruler of his, not even a sign of him (by which he can be inferred). He is the cause, the Lord of all Lords of the organs. He has no progenitor nor is there anyone who is his Lord.'

JnaniYoga
There is a cycle within the process of Self Realisation . This cycle cannot be altered, it must be accepted. Do not resist the cycle as resistance will cause unnecessary pain and suffering . The cycle is outlined here:
•An experience of ignorance, lost in the illusion of the world, despairing and hopeless. An absolute forgetfulness of all that is real.
•Something happens, as if by accident, and God is remembered. A humility and reverence is experienced. Hope is restored. Faith is stronger. The need for realisations comes back. You realise something new.
•Overly confident. Believing who I am now is forever. Complacency and arrogance are strong. A lack of gratitude towards one's preceptor. A feeling that God is unnecessa ry. A belief that one has finished, and the goal has been reached.
Each individual will flow through the cycle, sometimes effortlessly, sometimes painfully. Try to remember the cycle, and that it is inevitable. Remembering will aid you through, and make the cycle less painful.

Bhakti Yoga
I prayed and now it's over, my answer has yet to come, and all I know is possible for the earth to overcome. The problems we are facing are created by mankind, the ignorance is dumbfounding and has created such a bind. The world has lost its cycle, its cycle of birth and death. It holds on to things forever and forgets to have trust and faith. The faith has waned and wilted for year upon year, and friends, all that was needed was to turn to you, oh Brahman my dear.

Karma Yoga
CYCLE
What is a cycle? A cycle is an evolutionary process that goes through stages, which are necessary for anything to evolve, grow and transform. Nature has a

cycle of seasons, which are critical to its evolution. Souls also have a cycle, which are also critical to their growth. Do not resist a soul's cycle, just as nature does not resist its own seasons.

Questions

1.Do you recognise the cycle of Self Realisation?
2.Do you accept it cannot be altered?
3.How do you resist the cycle?
4.Share your experience of all three seasons within this cycle.
5.How do you deal with your ignorance?
6.Do you immerse yourself in your realisations?
7.When you witness your arrogance, do you want to be rid of it?
8.Are you aware that you are in an evolutionary process, like the seasons?
9.Do you realise this cycle is critical for your growth?
10.How do you not resist the cycles, and accept them in daily life?

Today: Cultivate humility and turn to Brahman and have faith and trust in him.

Verse 10

Verse
'May that only God, who spontaneously covers himself with the products of prakriti or nature, just as a spider does with the threads (drawn from its own navel) grant us identity with Brahman.'

JnaniYoga
Knowing now that the soul's cycle is critical to its evolution will make one feel afraid. A healthy fear though, that what will happen when one continues to fall into ignorance, or arrogance. Practice accepting that some fears are healthy and aid caution.

Bhakti Yoga
Don't leave me now it's over, turn to you I must, all the doors have closed now of greed and desires and lust.

Karma Yoga
INSECURITY
Insecurity is a panic, an explosion of fearful energy from within towards the belief in loosing something, or someone. In relation to God this is normal and acceptable. And keeps you on your toes, and vigilant at all times. Sometimes it's consuming,

but other times it is mainly just a knowing inside that it is possible to loose your connection with God. It keeps you maintaining a level of effort with your spiritual practice.

Questions
1.Are you afraid?
2.Can you tell the difference between healthy and unhealthy fear?
3.What is caution and how is it relevant?
4.Do you ever experience insecurity?
5.Can you describe how it feels?
6.What is insecurity in relation to God?
7.What is human insecurity?
8.How do these insecurities compare?
9.Do you ever get consumed by insecurity?
10.How can insecurity towards God be helpful?

Today: Know that when you let go of your desires an insecurity will follow, but with faith and trust everything will be ok.

Verse 11

Verse
'God, who is one only, is hidden in all beings. He pervades all and he is the inner soul of all beings. He presides over all actions and all beings dwell in him. He is the witness and he is the pure consciousness. He is alone or single and is devoid of all qualities.'

JnaniYoga
The insecurity that one feels on a human level towards a loved one, or a situation, does not compare with insecurity felt on a Divine level. Think about it logically and/or emotionally. Do you need God more than anything, if the only reason we exist is to serve God through knowing our Self? Why do you put so much energy into fearing the loss of a loved one, is a loved one not a companion, a friend on this journey? Can they really help you to get home? Are they not in your life to enjoy, love and care about? But is not their happiness what's important? If they want to leave you, is it not an expression of love to let go, to not hold on so tightly? Are their wishes less important than yours? Do not waste time fearing the departure of a loved one, enjoy them.

Bhakti Yoga
How could I ever leave you my child, I am always there. Here and there, always so intrinsically inseparable. I am woven into the fabric of all your being and more.

·Chapter VI·

My child it saddens me greatly that you would lose all trust. Do you not realise I am always, always with you. Myself, it never abandons I could not ever imagine such. This yearning in your being deep down at your very core, is my voice as it beckons you to lust my child, to lust. To lust for all my thoughts now, and all my feelings too, my actions are also available for you my child, for you, for you. I beckon you to join me in this home made up for two, and when my child you join me the two will become one. There is no us or we dear one in this the eternal home. The us and we are past, gone, and replaced by a single or alone.

Karma Yoga
ALONE
The fundamental truth is that there is only ever really you and God. And beyond that the realised truth is that there is only God. So, why waste time believing you are not alone? You are alone, but you are alone with God. And, until you realise your Self as God, God is your only company, companion and friend. Anything else is transitory and impermanent. Therefore, alone means standing next to God by yourself, and accepting that this is the only real certainty in life.

Questions
1.Describe insecurity towards a human.
2.Logically and emotionally how does it make you feel and think?
3.Do you not need God more than anything?
4.Why do you put so much energy into loosing loved ones?
5.Is a loved one not a companion to make the journey more enjoyable?
6.Do you let go of people too easily, or hold on too tightly?
7.What is this fundamental truth about you and God?
8.Can you imagine that there is only God?
9.'You are alone with God.' What does this mean?
10.How can you be alone with God better?

Today: Know that to be alone, is to be with God only.

Verse 12

Verse
'He is the one controller of the inactive many. He makes the one seed manifold. The wise, who perceive him within their self, to them belongs eternal happiness, not to others.'

JnaniYoga
Being so close to home now, everything seems so much harder. The resistance, inside and outside is getting stronger, faith is waning, problems are arising as

if from nowhere. This is the time where one has to stand firm, the foundation of learning that you have built your journey upon can take the weight of this seemingly real storm. The storm is not real, just like it has never been real. This is just your ego fighting harder to survive, to live. Stay strong now, don't give in, fight harder, stay true to everything you have learnt and understood.

Bhakti Yoga
Breathe a sigh of relief dear one, alone are we once more. My mind has become so clear now, and my heart no longer filled with fear. Them, they and others have returned now to the place whence they came from , to fill a void of never-ending loneliness in the global stratosphere. And when one day they miss you and their hearts are devoid of truth, them, they and the others will join you in the eternal happiness of this the Ultimate Truth.

Karma Yoga
EXAMPLE
Someone is watching you from somewhere, they are observing your every thought, word and deed. Looking to see if what you are doing is worth attempting for themselves. They are looking to you, and how they perceive your strengths and weaknesses, to gauge whether or not your hard work has paid off. You are an example. An example is something someone tries before they buy the real thing. Be a good example.

Questions
1.How does it feel to be getting close to home?
2.Do things seem harder at the moment?
3.Is your resistance getting stronger?
4.How are you standing firm on your foundation?
5.What is your foundation?
6.Can you accept your ego is trying to stay alive?
7.Who is watching your example?
8.What are you an example of?
9.What are your strengths and weaknesses?
10.Are you a good example?

Today: Be an example of Truth today, and know that others will follow.

Verse 13

Verse
'He is the eternal among the eternals and the intelligent among all that are

·Chapter VI·

intelligent. Through one he grants the desires of the many. He who has known Him, the cause of all, who is to be comprehended by Sankhya (philosophy) and yoga (religious discipline), is freed from all fetters.'

JnaniYoga

You have relied so long now on your preceptor, and their example. But, now you have to bring yourself forward, you have to show your light. You have to rely on your own light also. It is no longer an option to act like a child with your preceptor, you are so close to your goal. You have to rise up to the challenge and be accountable for yourself also. How are you accountable for who you are and what you know?

Bhakti Yoga

How could one believe that the eternal and ultimate Truth could ever be understood by mind alone. What ignorance brings you to this place of arrogance? Are you to spend all time , are you to fill all space with such nonsense? Did I not create you in the image of God, did I not place within you a spark of myself. Do you deem me to be as insignificant as once you had become? You took yourself to a place of loneliness, despair and hopelessness. Do you think that anything so insignificant could alone remove the veil. No my child, no. The mind alone cannot comprehend me. I am not to be realised by mind alone. The heart of the matter can, and will transform the mind alone. But, how does one find the heart? With the mind of God. This quandary is what you must conquer, you must face this challenge head on, and all that you will need now will be given freely with my grace, my grace, my grace.

Karma Yoga

BALANCE

The weight of God's responsibility is equal to the weight of your own. If you place these two weights on a set of scales would they be in balance? Balance is about the head and the heart having an equal relationship within your Self. God is responsible for your heart, you are responsible for your head. Simply put, God provides the energy of love, and you provide the vessel. The love pours easily into a clean vessel. How clean is your vessel?

Questions

1.Do you rely on your preceptor?
2.How is your preceptor an example?
3.Do you show your own light?
4.How often do you actually rely on your own light?
5.How are you accountable?

·Chapter VI·

6.Who are you, and what do you know?
7.What is God's responsibility to you?
8.How are you being responsible for yourself?
9.How does God love you?
10.How clean is your vessel?

Today: Remember always, mind alone cannot conquer the realisations required to know God. Mind and heart must work together to manifest the Grace needed to find God.

Verse 14

Verse
'The sun does not shine there, neither the moon, nor the stars. There, these lightnings do not shine, how then this fire? When he shines everything shines after him. By his light all this shines.'

JnaniYoga
Give your mind to God, there is no longer a real need to be in control of your mind. The journey is almost completed, you have everything you have needed inside you. So, let go and trust in God. Let him take your mind, and do whatever he needs to do. This is the final straight you're on now, remember even though it seems harder it's only because your ego knows you're getting closer and wants you to stop. Focus on God, remember why you are doing this, remember all the good times, remember how great you are. And just let go.

Bhakti Yoga
This mind of yours is indeed troublesome. It creates so many avenues of discontent. It travels so far and so wide in search of peace and happiness. But, pray, what does it ever find, what answers does it ever reach? Round and round it goes, up and down, near and far and still yet it refuses to stop, relentless it is, it is relentless. Stop, just know exactly where you are and rest your mind in that spot. Look north, look south, east and west and tell me what you see there.
Mindless noise, chattering, images and more, and of what use are these things to you, to me? Not any use you say, not any use. So why, oh why, do you continue, when will you stop? Stop I must, to grow, to see, to feel exactly what I must. That nothing can be sought by mind alone, nothing can be found. I'm tired now defeated at last, my heart has conquered all. It tells me of a place deep inside that aches and yearns, a place that I am afraid. A place within that tells me nothing of what is to become, a noise, a sound, a pain I feel that reaches beyond my mind where only you can know what's there. God, you know me more than myself. Trust I must

in you alone, to guide me here inside this place, I feel so unsure of where I'm going in here. There is no darkness, or seeming light, but still I feel afraid. I fear the unknown of such a thing that only you can help me face. My fear subsides, and light shines forth inside this place of mine, the fire of my soul is alight with you, God, forever more. A light so bright, a fire so alive that my fear is no longer real. I cannot but help admire you now for your wisdom, your awareness and your appeal.

Karma Yoga
APPEAL
You are attractive, yes you. The Self that you have grown to know through devotion, study and helping those in need. You are drawn towards yourself. You have appeal, something that you want, and desire. Your Self.

Questions
1.Can you give your mind to God?
2.How do you try to be in control of your mind?
3.Do you believe you have everything you need inside you?
4.Can you let go more, and trust God more?
5How can you focus on God?
6.Describe the good times you've had thus far.
7.Can you let go?
8.Are you attractive?
9.Do you feel drawn, attracted towards your Self?
10.Do you desire your Self?

Today: Tell yourself that the heart is much more appealing than the mind alone.

Verse 15

Verse
'He is the one Soul (Hamsa) destroyer of ignorance in the midst of the world. He alone is the fire which is seated in water. Knowing him truly one overcomes death. There is no other path for liberation.'

JnaniYoga
So, you can experience the joy of being your Self. There is a deep sense of realisation that you have found what you were always looking for. But the past, which is still a clear memory inside, is pulling on you. The attachments that once felt so real, the desires that once felt so painful, the relationships that once felt so

necessary. The memories are starting to reappear, the illusion of their fulfilment flooding back into your heart. So, now what do you do, how do you deal with these memories? Allow the memories to fill your heart, and be honest with yourself, pray for the strength to see them as they really were, and not how you wanted them to be. Be honest, and then let them go, remember they are in the past, and remind yourself of everything in your present, remind yourself of God and all will be well. It is necessary to look back before you go forward.

Bhakti Yoga
The loneliness in here God, it aches so very much. There is no one left to see myself in, no one left at all. I am alone, all by myself with you right by my side so why, oh why, oh why God, do I not feel alone is good? I ache, I strain, I feel now so lonely in my core, a pain that stretches on now and will cease no more, no more. The floodgates I have opened to a heart designed just for me, the Self inside is lonesome for all I need to be and see. I know not of your plan now for me, for me, for me, it saddens me so much now that to go back is not an option for thee.

Karma Yoga
ACHE
A physical sensation, a feeling that grows within the heart, pulling, stretching your Self towards more and more of the Divine. A real, painful heartfelt agony that acknowledges that you are not yet there, but ever so close it hurts. It pains to be so close, and yet unable to reach out and touch the hand of God. This pain can be confusing, and at this stage must not be confused with the ache that arises for physical human contact. This Divine ache is felt in the heart, at the centre of the chest, just right of the physical heart.

Questions
1.Do you ever experience joy about being your Self?
2.Have you found what you were looking for?
3.Are you being pulled back by your past?
4.What are the past memories?
5.Can you see the memories for what they really were?
6.Can you let your memories go?
7.How do you remind yourself of God?
8.Do you feel pulled towards God?
9.How does it feel to be so close, but still out of reach?
10.Describe the ache in your heart for God.

Today: Know only God can be your friend, your mother, your father, your

·Chapter VI·

husband, your wife, your son, your daughter.

Verse 16

Verse
'He creates the universe and knows the universe. He is his own source. He is all-knowing, and he is the time of time (destroyer of time). He is endowed with all qualities of perfection. He knows everything in detail. He is the master of nature and men and the Lord of the gunas. He is the cause of the bondage, the existence and the liberation of the world.'

JnaniYoga
This is a genuinely enjoyable lesson. The opportunity to reach out and help just one person whom you deem to be in need. This is so different from sharing with others, it gains you valuable insight into the connection between two souls when in service of God. There are few things on this spiritual journey that compare to the amazing feeling when a true connection is made. Two complete strangers, Atmans merged together as one, a memory of home rushes back, the oneness of creation. Reach out and help just one soul who needs you.

Bhakti Yoga
You'll take great care of me God, I know you always will. I trust you to the ends of the Earth, until my heart beats still. I pray for now and always that we can soldier on, together now we must God, for all the Souls have gone, they have gone. Their hearts are lost in torment, toils and troubles they continue to face. I cannot face the task on my own God, to you I must turn now and embrace, embrace, embrace.

Karma Yoga
EMBRACE
Wrap your arms around a soul and hold them tight in your warmth, your softness, your light. Emit this energy through your being and into theirs. Don't be shy, be God. Embrace a soul with all that you are, fold yourself around them, in them, behind and in front of them . Immerse them in who you are.

Questions
1.Are you looking forward to helping an individual soul?
2.How do you distinguish need?
3.How does it feel to be connected to another soul?
4.Do you feel like you're serving God?
5.Can you feel your Atmans merge together as one?
6.Can you feel an awareness of home beckoning you?

·Chapter VI·

7.How can you embrace another soul?
8.How can you emit your energy towards them?
9.Do you experience yourself as shy or confident when serving God?
10.Describe being God.

Today: Take a step, just one step, to helping another soul who is less fortunate than yourself.

Verse 17

Verse
'He is like himself, immortal and abides in the form of ruler. He is the all-knowing, all-pervading protector of the world, the eternal ruler. No one else is able to rule over it.'

JnaniYoga
Every step now is taking you ever closer, every lesson moving you nearer to him. You can feel his breath now, you can hear his heartbeat, he is becoming real to you. Just like a person you can make out his outline, his shadow, his smell. The awe you must feel is overwhelming. Nothing could prepare you for this experience. The reality is far greater than what you imagined it to be. You see how small you have become, small enough to fit in his hand. And yet, within the smallness, you feel bigger than you've ever felt. Enjoy being small.

Bhakti Yoga
We must take our steps together Lord, watch over me your child. I beg for your forgiveness for my mistakes, my failings, my doubts, my fears, my toils. There is no greater solace now for me. My heart is filled with so much respect for my master who has killed , he has killed the fear of ego, of abandonment and doubt, that plagued me for so many moons Lord that my heart began to shout. It shouted with despair Lord, with absolute abandonmen,t a sin I can never forgive myself, a creation of a true resentment. I prostrate now before you Lord, my being humbled by your Grace, your supreme abundance has renewed my faith , my faith, my faith.

Karma Yoga
HUMBLED
Oh! My God, I feel absolutely bowled over, knocked off my feet at how magnificent you are. I can't believe it, it's like I've just stumbled into a fairytale, and all the stories that could only be imagined have just materialised in front of me. You are too great, too magnificent , too amazing. I am unworthy of looking into your eyes, your presence humbles me.

·Chapter VI·

Questions

1.Do you feel close to God?
2.What is it like to be close to him?
3.How is he becoming more real to you?
4.Does it feel like a real relationship?
5.Has anything really prepared you for this experience?
6.How did you imagine it would be?
7.Do you feel small and insignificant compared to him?
8.Are you experiencing your greatness within the experience of being small?
9. How magnificent is God?
10.How humbled are you by his presence?

Today: Cultivate humility to the Lord, Master of the supreme universe.

Verse 18

Verse
'Let me, desirous of liberation, resort to the God for refuge whose light turns the intellect towards the Atman, who at the commencement of creation created Brahma and who gave the Vedas to him.'

JnaniYoga
The enormity of God's grace that all he ever taught has remained, and stood the test of time for over five thousand years. All these transitory teachings, worldly technologies, responses to all of life's problems that rise up through time, and constantly change. Our individual and collective minds, they change so often, it is painful to watch how taken in people become. Oh yes, this will work. Only to have it swept away through time. Only God's knowledge remains and always will.

Bhakti Yoga
I am so glad that I gave myself to thee, that you could take such a wretch as myself and transform me anew into a creation of wonderment and awe. That I am you and you are me, and that the me that is you has no longer to fear the darkness, the pain, the loneliness. But, to stand ever so tall in the glory of your ever greatness. All you are, all you will ever be is right there before me. All along it resided patiently for thousands of years, never changing, never leaving, staying in one place at all times. If only I could turn to you and return your grace. If only I could remove from you the veil upon my face. If only I could reach you and show you who I am. If you could know I knew you, and your Divine plan.

·Chapter VI·

Karma Yoga
VEDAS
God has communicated directly to all of his children through the scriptures. We spend so much time trying new fads, and trendy ideas. Trends that change with time. All of our problems can, and must, be solved by referring to God's words, his Grace bestowed upon us through the Vedas.

Questions
1.What has God taught us?
2.Have God's teachings stood the test of time?
3.What are the transitory teachings that fail to withstand time?
4.How do you adhere to these impermanent trends?
5.Do you feel silly at how easily you fall for the latest fads?
6.How does God's knowledge remain with us?
7.What are scriptures?
8.Do you refer to scriptures to solve problems?
9.What else do you refer to for advice and guidance?
10.What are the Vedas?

Today: Remember that this search has been continuing for thousands of years. Nothing has changed, or ever will. There are no new ideas, concepts or philosophies. All was Brahman, all is Brahman and all will ever be Brahman.

Verse 19

Verse
'Who is without parts, without action, who is tranquil, blameless, spotless, the supreme bridge of immortality and who is like the fire that has consumed its fuel (to him I go for refuge).'

JnaniYoga
Everything has taken so much effort until this point. You now realise that the effort was, and is, unnecessary. Everything you are God willed into existence, and with you he sent a book of his knowledge and wisdom, a book that will make everything from this point easier, and effortless. Study the Vedas, and refer to them religiously to solve all of life's problems.

Bhakti Yoga
Atman is without face , without hands, feet or form. There is a place deep within,

·Chapter VI·

inside your very being that resides without effort, without cause, without reason. Know this place exists at all time s, and no matter what you do it always, always will.

Karma Yoga
REASON
We only live out this meaningless existence to realise the meaningful within it. We are born to know ourselves alone, who we truly are behind , or within, the facade of our ego's disguise. Through fear we lose our realness, and fall into the darkness of ignorance . Through love we find ourselves, and merge with the light of knowledge. Our only reason for existing was this, our only reason, meaning factually, nothing else is real.

Questions
1.Describe the effort and hard work that has enabled you to reach this point.
2.Can you see the effort was only an illusion?
3.What is meant by: 'Everything you are, God willed into existence.'
4.Did God send you his knowledge and wisdom when you were born?
5.Do you study the Vedas?
6.How do you realise the meaningful within existence?
7.Are you born alone to know yourself?
8.How does fear take you into the darkness of ignorance?
9.Has love merged you with the light of knowledge?
10.Is nothing else real?

Today: Know there is nothing you can do that cannot be done.

Verse 20

Verse
'Only when men shall roll up the sky like skin, will there be an end of misery, unless God has first been known.'

JnaniYoga
Time has passed, and you have spent some time now alone with God digging deeper down into the depths of consciousness. Exploring yourself, and your own relationship with God. But, now you are coming out of this alone time you will need your preceptor. You will be feeling a dull ache, an emptiness, a feeling of having left God. Remember your relationship with your preceptor and reconnect to them. Share with them where you have been, and all that you have learnt.

·Chapter VI·

Let them witness your growth, and reflect on your transformation.

Bhakti Yoga
This all seems so inadequate, so meaningless, so unnecessary. A dialogue between me and who, who am I to speak of this place we know so well, a place where no one goes to, it feels so painful. I know not why I do this, for you I feel I must. I ramble on incessantly, to build trust upon trust upon trust. I cannot imagine ever a day when this will be so, my heart it pains me so madly, but carry on reluctantly I must. There seems to be a void now, a place beckoning deep inside, a wrenching of my soul I feel, a deep need to just abide. I need to feel you close now, a journey I must make, to see your Supreme face upon all the souls I take. I will take them to the corners of consciousness Divine, to bask in your Supremeness with their hands in yours, in mine. I will show them all the beauty, the richness you showed me, all of your light and guidance that has been so much help to me.

Karma Yoga
SUPREMENESS
The best, and most superior version of SELF. Remember your preceptor will always be superior. Don't fall back into complacency and arrogance. Recognise they are the highest, acknowledge their Supremeness.

Questions
1.How has it been for you being alone with God?
2.How deep have you dug into consciousness?
3.What is your relationship with God like now?
4.Do you feel an awareness of needing your preceptor?
5.Are you feeling alone, an emptiness at having left God?
6.Can you share your growth with your preceptor, if so how?
7.Can you accept now that one's preceptor is highest?
8.How is your preceptor superior to you?
9.Do you acknowledge their supremeness?
10.Find a way to revere your preceptor. What is that way?

Today: I want to share with you that only God can perform the miracles required to liberate you from the bondage of Self unconsciousness.

Verse 21

Verse
'Having realised Brahman, through the power of his penance and through

·Chapter VI·

the grace of God, the wise Svetasvatara expounded well to the highest order of sannyasins the truth of that supremely holy Brahman resorted to by all the seers.'

JnaniYoga
This is the first of the final three lessons, and as such must be taken seriously. Your approach to your preceptor is of utmost importance. You must go to them with humility, reverence and respect. It is so easy to fall at the end, to walk up the Mountain of Divine Remembrance, and stumble. The peak of this mountain, just as with all mountains, is out of view. It is clouded with a fog of fear. The fear is even greater still, and even though the awareness of the unrealness is shouting out in a loud, clear voice, within your heart, your mind is also shouting, 'Stop, go back down, give up, it's too hard, you'll never do it.' Remember, Brahman is only expounded to the highest order of sannyasins. A sannyasin only comes into being when all that was believed to be real is renounced. Challenge everything perceived still to be real in your life, and renounce its authenticity. Your preceptor will give you the Grace that only he can bestow on you in this, one of your most difficult lessons.

Bhakti Yoga
I will take you by the hand now and hold onto you I must, so that you can cultivate a relationship with the God that you must trust. And trust will not come so easy, for such a boon comes at a price, you must renounce your will now, and for this God will entice.

Karma Yoga
BOONS
Vaulting forwards on your path. Jumping over obstacles along the way, destroying the ego. These are all gifts from God, and through the Grace of your preceptor are plentiful. These gifts are boons, boons you so desperately need.

Questions
1.How does it feel to be only three lessons away from success?
2.Are you taking these lessons seriously?
3.How are you approaching your preceptor?
4.Do you know of this mountainous peak clouded with fear?
5.Can you hear your inner Self?
6.How does your mind try to prevent you from continuing your climb?
7.Are you of the highest order or sannyasins?
8.Are you willing to renounce all that was once real?
9. Do you experience your preceptor's Grace?

·Chapter VI·

10.Have you received boons from your preceptor?

Today: To trust God you must renounce all that you believe to be real.

Verse 22

Verse
'This highest mystery or secret in the Vedanta, expounded in a former age, should not be given to one whose passions have not been subdued, nor to one who is not a worthy son, nor to an unworthy disciple.'

JnaniYoga
Boons, the Grace bestowed by the preceptor to one's disciple, are not freely given they must be earned. Only the knower of Brahman can determine what is worthy of receiving his Grace. What determines a worthy disciple? Here is a comprehensive list, in order of importance, of what a preceptor looks for in a disciple:
•Respect towards the preceptor.
•Humility towards the preceptor.
•Following the preceptor's teachings.
•Sharing the preceptor's message.
•Protecting the preceptor.
•Studying scriptures.
•Cultivating love and devotion through Bhakti yoga.
•Serving those less fortunate.
•Being a good example.

Cultivate the points above, start with the first and work your way through the list until you are exemplary at each one.

Bhakti Yoga
This task will take you to places where he will seem appealing, to territories and terrains that appear impossible. And you will falter, you will resist, you will turn your back upon God and deny his very exist ence. Everything you deemed to be reality will be challenged, and the old constructs that felt safe will be destroyed. And every part of your being will scream out in agony, the pain and suffering that once felt so excruciating will rear its ugly head. And you will cry, you will beg for ignorance once more. But know this with all certainty from one who has conquered, that nowhere backwards is anywhere at all. Forwards holds all and everything - and forwards you must go, you must push, you must push, you must push.

·Chapter VI·

Karma Yoga
DISCIPLE
A disciple is an individual who is strict with their spiritual practice and follows their preceptor's teachings to the best of their ability. This individual may state that they are worthy of calling themselves a disciple.

Questions
1.How are you earning boons?
2.Do you try to steal or manipulate boons?
3.What determines a worthy disciple?
4.Are you a worthy disciple of your preceptor?
5.How do you feel about the comprehensive list?
6.Have you cultivated any of the points?
7.What is your strongest point?
8.How are you dealing with your weaknesses?
9.Are you strict with your spiritual practice?
10.Are you worthy to call yourself a disciple?

Today: This is a painful journey, one of untold suffering. But hold onto the moments, the glimpses of sheer bliss, because they are worth every scar, every wound, every bleed.

Verse 23

Verse
'If these truths have been told to a high-souled one, who has supreme devotion to God and as much devotion to his Guru or preceptor as to God, then only, they will shine forth, then only, they will shine forth indeed.'

JnaniYoga
Do you want to call yourself a high-souled one? Do you believe that you have earned that title? Are there flaws in your study, obstacles you have avoided? How honest are you, or have you been throughout your study? The Svetasvatara Upanishad finally reaches its conclusion. Svetasvatara asks that one who has supreme devotion to God, and as much devotion to their preceptor as to God, will succeed. Observe your relationship with your preceptor. Svetasvatara is telling you that you must see him as equal to God. Your preceptor stands between you and God. Only he decides if you are worthy of entering God's kingdom. Challenge your perception of your preceptor, ask yourself what is real.

·Chapter VI·

Bhakti Yoga
I'm tired now dear high-souled one, a rest here awhile I must. My heart has shared its last now, as I hand the gauntlet over to you, my love, so you can build your trust. The work is yours my child, as you study, worship and lust, for God dear one is waiting for your heart, your soul, your trust. Your heart must open slowly, but a wide and vast space, to be filled with an abundance of beauty to bring tears rolling down your face. The beauty I do speak of here is like none you have ever known, but the ramblings on these pages have served for you to be shown. I pray for your forgiveness to the God that I do own, for once you realise your heart, dear one, we are never truly really ever alone.

Karma Yoga
HIGH-SOULED ONE
All individual souls are born into the cycle of karma. Freedom of karma is the goal. Every soul is born with a level of realisation from previous births. This lifetime serves to destroy the ego, break free from karma, and realise one's True Nature. A high-souled one is either born with a high level of Realisations from previous births, or works hard in this birth, and reaps the rewards of Realisations by reaching a higher level. All souls are at different levels due to their unique karma. A high-souled one is an individual whose soul, the Self within, is advanced, and close to Brahman. This closeness is experienced only through great effort, and an abundance of hard work.

Questions
1.Do you want to call yourself a high-souled one?
2.Have you worked hard and put in great effort?
3.Have you avoided any obstacles along your path?
4.Are you honest with God about your lessons and your study?
5.Do you have supreme devotion to God?
6.Are you devoted to your preceptor as much as you are to God?
7.Do you see God and your preceptor as one?
8.Who is a high-souled one?
9.Do you feel close to Brahman?
10.Are you Brahman?

Today: A high-souled one can only call themselves thus if they take responsibility for the hard work it takes to reach a home where nobody knows but I.

·Chapter VI·

Main Point of Chapter VI

THE RELATIONSHIP WITH DEVOTION TO GOD FROM THE VIEWPOINT OF YOUR SELF

The main point conveyed to you throughout Chapter VI is about your relationship with your devotion to God from the viewpoint of your SELF. The SELF inside all beings must cultivate a deeper, more meaningful relationship with Brahman for Self Realisation to deepen. This relationship is the final stage of Self Realisation . This relationship starts with an awareness of Brahman himself, and your need to hold onto him tightly.

The process now has its goal, and the steps to realise this goal are as follows:

a)Submerge yourself in the energy of love and devotion.
b)Acknowledge the power of your preceptor.
c)Share your preceptor's message.
d)Praise God.
e)Relinquish your ego.
f)Become God's servant.
g)Share your path with others.
h)Accept the three stage cycle within the Self Realisation process.
i)Accept having a healthy fear of losing God.
j)Be alone with God.
k)Be a good example.
l)Be a clean vessel for God's lov e.
m)Desire your Self.
n)Ache for God.
o)Embrace an individual soul.
p)Be humbled by God's presence.
q)Learn the Vedas.
r)Only love is real.
s)Acknowledge your preceptor's Supremeness.
t)Receive your preceptor's Grace.
u)Cultivate the art of being a disciple.
v)Become a high-souled one.

This chapter outlines, and clearly guides you, towards an ever greater experience of Brahman. The chapter shows you how to realise you are one with Brahman, which is the ultimate goal of the journey of Self Realisation . It is the final stage, and therefore for all things worthy it requires great effort.

If you wish to find out more about Satguru Sri Ramana Devi;
Darshan, Upanishad and Self Realsation in the West, then
please contact us or visit Sri Ramana's website:
www.sriramanadevi.org

Satguru Sri Ramana Devi

If you wish to find out more about Satguru Sri Ramana Devi, then please contact us or visit Her website

www.sriramanadevi.org
info@sriramanadevi.org
01706 601 644